SO GOD MADE A DOG

SO GOD MADE A DOG

90
Devotions for Dog People

WORTHY®
Inspired

Published by Worthy Inspired, an imprint of Worthy Publishing Group, a division of Worthy Media, Inc., One Franklin Park, 6100 Tower Circle, Suite 210, Franklin, TN 37067.

WORTHY is a registered trademark of Worthy Media, Inc.

HELPING PEOPLE EXPERIENCE THE HEART OF GOD

eBook available wherever digital books are sold.

Scripture quotations are taken from the following sources: The Holy Bible, New International Version®, NIV® Copyright © 1973, 1978, 1984, 2011 by Biblica, Inc.® All rights reserved worldwide. The Holy Bible, New King James Version® (NKJV). Copyright © 1982 by Thomas Nelson, Inc. The Holy Bible, English Standard Version® (ESV®), copyright © 2001 by Crossway Bibles, a publishing ministry of Good News Publishers. The New American Standard Bible® (NASB), Copyright © 1960, 1962, 1963, 1968, 1971, 1972, 1973, 1975, 1977, 1995 by The Lockman Foundation. The Holy Bible, New Living Translation (NLT) copyright © 1996, 2004, 2007 by Tyndale House Foundation. Used by permission of Tyndale House Publishers Inc., Carol Stream, Illinois 60188. The Message (MSG). Copyright © 1993, 1994, 1995, 1996, 2000, 2001, 2002. Used by permission of NavPress Publishing Group. All rights reserved.

For foreign and subsidiary rights, contact rights@worthypublishing.com

ISBN: 978-1-68397-026-2

Compiled by Barbara Farmer
Cover Design: Melissa Reagan

Printed in the United States of America

17 18 19 20 21 LBM 9 8 7 6 5 4 3 2 1

For dog people and the dogs they belong to.

Charlie and the Kitten

Instead, be kind to each other, tenderhearted,
forgiving one another, just as God
through Christ has forgiven you.

EPHESIANS 4:32 NLT

The first meeting between Charlie and the new kitten was, to put it mildly, explosive. The kitten, removed from her mother far too early, arrived at her new home a terrified ninja, lashing out at anything and everything with razor-sharp kitten-claws. This included, unfortunately, Charlie's nose.

Charlie yelped but resisted retaliation. A large German Shepherd-Collie mix, Charlie had a soft heart and a kind spirit. He seemed to sense the kitten wasn't mean, just scared. He never held the injured nose against her. Instead, he became her surrogate mom.

At first, he lay quietly next to the big blanket-filled box that kept the kitten, now named Tillie, secure. Tillie remained in the box about a week, being hand-fed, with tenuous excursions around the den or patio. Charlie almost never left her side during these trips, although he stayed out of the reach of her claws for a few days.

Soon, Tillie realized that the other warm, furry creature in her new home wasn't going to hurt her, and the two bonded. Charlie replaced the box as Tillie's favorite bed. She would clamber up on Charlie's side and fall fast asleep. Charlie would peer at her, sigh, and lie still until Tillie woke with a startled mew. He would then nuzzle her to give comfort. As she grew older, she would answer by kneading his back with tiny paws that barely penetrated his thick fur.

When their owner worked in his garage, Charlie would stretch out on the cool concrete, Tillie tucked between his front legs or curled against his tummy. The older she got, the more remarkable this picture became as Charlie would sometimes wrap his long legs around the tall, lanky cat, hugging her as if she were a child. Tillie never objected, and only occasionally looked annoyed, the way a teenager might when Mother insists on one more public kiss.

The tenderness between them never abated, and as Tillie became an adult, they would romp around the backyard like old friends, chasing birds and squirrels—which they never caught—and tennis balls—which they did occasionally. Tillie could stab a tennis ball with her claws and fling it halfway across the yard. The sharp claws that had once wounded Charlie now created hours of unbridled joy.

Watching them one summer afternoon, their owner commented, "Makes me think the lamb really will lie down with the lion."

When we embrace forgiveness and compassion toward others, great friendships will emerge. And, as Charlie and Tillie found out, endless possibilities can come from those bonds. Most importantly, we can begin to see others as God sees them—as His children, beloved and cherished, just as we are.

Lord, revive Your love that lives in my heart.
Help me show compassion and friendship toward all,
for we are all Your children. Amen.

Cornbread

*We know that in all things God works for the good
of those who love him, who have been called
according to his purpose.*

ROMANS 8:28 NIV

One of my earliest memories is discovering a box on our porch one cold winter morning when I was five years old. I clasped my hands together. "Someone left us a present!"

Mama opened the screen door and looked inside the box. "A puppy." She lifted him, and he snuggled under her chin. "He's cold."

Daddy looked over her shoulder and shook his head. "He's all ears."

"Can we keep it?" My voice lifted. Mama's eyes met Daddy's, and after a few seconds, he nodded.

Later that day, I sat next to the heater in the kitchen cuddling my new friend and tried out different names. When Mama removed an iron skillet from the oven, the pup started howling, and I noticed the color of his coat matched the cornbread's crust. "His name is Cornbread."

Cornbread grew, and his long ears almost touched the ground, which caused many to speculate his daddy was a Basset Hound. Every afternoon we'd walk first to Mrs. Harris's home, as she often had warm cookies waiting, and after that we'd stop and see Mr. Elliot. Our elderly neighbors enjoyed seeing Cornbread as much as I did.

When school started, I worried about Cornbread being lonely, but he continued to visit our friends. I'd jump off the school bus and rush across the street to Mr. Elliot who sat waiting in his lawn chair with his gnarled hand on Cornbread's head. The two spent many hours together. Cornbread seemed to have an instinct for the neighbor who needed his company the most. He lavished love on everyone else as well and he grew fat on the extra treats given to him, but he always returned to our house at the end of the day.

It's sad that someone abandoned a helpless puppy on a cold winter morning, but God used this tragic event to bless many. Who knows what the person's intent was, but God was able to use this incident for the good. I've had my own piteous moments too, but God knew the paths I would take and He made a plan to guide me back to Him.

The Lord can take anything, even our tragedies, and turn them into blessings. What could have been a disaster for Cornbread turned out to be a gift. God can transform our worst moments into miracles. Consider how He used the brutal crucifixion of His Son and turned it into a victory over death and made a way for all mankind to be saved. God's ways our higher than our ways, and even when it seems I've been abandoned, I know I can trust in Him.

Thank You, Father, for making all things work for Your good.
I know You will never abandon me,
and that You have good plans for my future. Amen.

Expectations and Inconsistencies

Out of the same mouth come praise and cursing.
My brothers and sisters, this should not be.
Can both fresh water and salt water flow from the same spring?

JAMES 3:10–11 NIV

Whenever Bear, our chocolate Labrador-American Pit Terrier, rides in the car and we slow down to speak with someone inside the open window of a building, he has certain expectations. Because of past experiences, Bear expects the person at the window will hand him a puppy cup full of creamy vanilla Dairy Queen soft serve ice cream when we reach them. Usually, Bear is correct about what he can expect, but not always.

The bank teller does not hand out puppy cups. Neither do the employees at the taco restaurant, nor does the pharmacist at the drug store. Each time we pull away from one of these places without his puppy cup, Bear looks at us as if to say we forgot something. His disappointment is evident. Bear's expectations were not met, and he can't understand what happened.

The difference between driving to an open window and receiving a puppy cup and going through the exact same motions and not receiving a puppy cup can be downright cruel. Who knows? This inconsistency could cause Bear to distrust and be disillusioned. But drive-through windows are not the only inconsistencies in life. People can also be inconsistent in their behavior and in their speech.

Each of us comes into relationships with expectations, especially if the person we interact with calls themself a believer. There are certain things we expect them to say and certain things we expect them to do. When we come face to face with inconsistencies, like Bear faces when the person inside the drive-through window does not give him a puppy cup, it can leave us confused, distrusting, and disillusioned. We expect one thing, but get something totally different.

Thinking about Bear's expectations regarding puppy cups got me thinking about my life story and what it says about me. Am I consistent in my message? Do people know what they will get when they enter into a conversation with me? Can others believe I'll do what I say I'll do? Am I consistent in my witness for God?

As the saying goes, the acorn doesn't fall far from the tree. If I am truly a child of the one true and living God, joint heirs with His Son, Jesus Christ, shouldn't my life reflect the image of my Father? Can people see Jesus in me by the way I live and the way I talk? I figure the best place for me to be is tucked under the branches of my Creator, raising my branches up to praise Him and imitate Him.

Father, help me be a consistent witness for You so that when others see me they will know I represent You and know what to expect because of that relationship. Amen.

Unyielding Sacrifice

*He will not let you stumble; the one who watches
over you will not slumber. Indeed, he who watches over
Israel never slumbers or sleeps.*

PSALM 121:3-4 NLT

If the U.S. military gave out purple hearts to our canine heroes, there's no doubt that Lucca would have earned one. The German Shepherd has won many awards for her gallantry in combat and deserves every one. She was also the first American dog ever to take home the prestigious Dickin Medal, instituted in 1943 to honor the work of animals in service to their countries.

One touching photo shows Lucca wearing the medal, standing tall and gazing into the eyes of an equally decorated marine. The scene is striking not because the marine is kneeling at eye-level with a dog. The scene doesn't pull on heart strings merely because Lucca only has three legs. No, it's the way the soldier looks at the dog. His gaze holds gratitude, and maybe a hit of admiration.

"I owe her my life," the marine said. Christopher, a gunnery sergeant, was Lucca's handler while she sniffed out roadside bombs. Perhaps no one knows better than he how many countless lives Lucca helped save during her tours in Iraq and Afghanistan.

Over the course of six years, this German Shepherd went on more than 400 missions. Christopher was with her for most of that time. Thanks to Lucca and Christopher, no soldier ever died under Lucca's watch. She did, however, lose her front leg to a bomb in Afghanistan. Lucca's injury and recovery touched many hearts.

Her story, however, points to more than canine bravery and devotion. In Lucca, we see traces of God's character and unwavering devotion to His children. Everywhere we look, God's handiwork raises voices in praise—creation magnifying its Creator. And creation, including dogs, whispers to the listening heart all about the character, trustworthiness, and goodness of God.

In Lucca, we see traces of God's overflowing faithfulness, a God who goes to incredible lengths to save us. Lucca's sacrifice echoes of an even greater sacrifice, one that has saved and continues to save countless lives. We're reminded of the God who sacrificed His Son so that we could live.

Through Jesus, God rescues us from death and brings us into new life. In Christ, we not only receive eternal life after our time on Earth ends, but we receive abundant life here and now—a rich and soul-satisfying life in relationship with God.

When I look into the eyes of a dog, I see shadows of another world, a world without harsh judgment and criticism. A world of total acceptance and love. Perhaps that's what Christopher saw that day when he looked in Lucca's eyes.

Lord Jesus, thank You for revealing Yourself to me through
Your creation, and help me reflect Your character
and life-changing love to everyone I meet. Amen.

I Want That One!

*You have been set apart as holy to the LORD your God,
and he has chosen you from all the nations
of the earth to be his own special treasure.*

DEUTERONOMY 14:2 NLT

Mama, please can I have one? Pleeeeease, Mama?"
I think every parent will know what I'm talking about when I say my son gave me the puppy dog eyes. That's the pleading look we get whenever our child encounters a dog, cat, gerbil, fish, or whatever else he or she wants to add to the family pet menagerie. Only the toughest most disciplined parent can resist those eyes. Why, I've seen my big strong contractor husband fizzle in mere seconds, and then I have two sets of puppy dog eyes to resist.

I love animals so that's not the problem, but *somebody* has to be the voice of reason before your family becomes like the ones featured on the evening news with fifty-five dogs or thirty-four cats.

Our four-year-old, Jeremy, had begged for a dog for many months, but we had waited until we thought he was mature enough to know how to treat a puppy with kindness and to help take care of one.

That day had arrived and my husband and I witnessed a scene of pure love as our overall-clad little boy knelt in the middle of a litter of active puppies. Tails wagged and tongues washed his arms as he hugged them close. Giggles filled the air as they all fought for his attention, knocking him over in their excitement.

They were what I'd call "a little of this and a little of that" dogs, with so many varieties in their heritage that it was impossible to determine their breed. I told Jeremy, "We can't adopt all of them, so you have to choose one."

His pick was the runt of the litter. Jeremy told me, "I'll take this one." And then he turned to the bright-eyed puppy in his arms and said, "You're going to be *my* dog now, and you're going to live with me."

I got Jeremy and the puppy settled in the car while my husband paid for the dog. And then Waggie Tail started his journey to his new home and family.

Just as Jeremy chose his puppy, God chose us to be part of His family. I'm grateful that there is no limit to His offer of salvation. And I'm thankful that when He looked into the sea of humanity and saw our flaws and scars it didn't matter, even if we were the runt of the litter. *He wanted us!* He saw us through His eyes of grace and said, "I want that one, and that one, and that one. I choose all of them." And then He paid the price so that we could belong to Him forever.

Father, thank You for choosing me
and for making me part of Your family. Amen.

Search and Retrieve

For this is what the Sovereign LORD says:
I myself will search and find my sheep.

EZEKIEL 34:11 NLT

He lost his ball," my brother-in-law announced when he returned from taking Fink, my English Springer Spaniel, for a run. "Not possible," I thought, looking down at my dog panting furiously, his long pink tongue lolling from one side of his mouth.

Springers are known for having good noses. Hunters choose them to flush out or retrieve game birds. Police train them to detect narcotics and explosives. You'll often see a Springer working at an airport baggage carousel. My dog would *never* lose his favorite ball. The out-of-breath dog in front of me would persist until he had found it.

The next day I returned to the area of long, unmown grass where the missing ball lay hidden. I bent down, lifted the chain from my dog's neck and over his long silky ears. "Go find your ball," I said softly.

Fink shot off, nose low to the ground. Barely visible in the tall grass, I could only see his tail held high, wagging rhythmically as he worked. Every so often he stopped, raised his head and looked back at me. "Find," I shouted. He set to work again. I waited. Even I began to have doubts. Suddenly, Fink began to circle quickly in one location. He stopped. The grass rustled. Next, he bounded towards me, leaping high into the air. In his mouth he held a bright green object—his beloved tennis ball. He dropped it at my feet and looked up expectantly. "Good boy," I praised, ruffling his ears. He picked up the ball, and dropped it again. He was ready to play.

Just the same, God diligently searches for lost sheep. Jesus, who took up the title of Good Shepherd, told a story about a lost sheep. The shepherd looked for that one sheep until he had found it. When he had tracked it down, the shepherd released it from the snares and lifted the sheep onto his shoulders and carried it home, rejoicing. We are that sheep. When we are lost, our heavenly Father never abandons His search for us. When we are rescued, there is great rejoicing in heaven.

When you can't find direction in life, the Good Shepherd promises to be with you. When your days are dark and frightening, God will lead you along the right paths. When you have strayed a long way from the Lord, He will help you find the route back home to Him. When circumstances have left you hurting, the Lord God will comfort you. When you are unable to carry on and want to give up, the Good Shepherd will lift you into His arms. Your heavenly Father delights in saving you from the snares of life.

*Lord and my Shepherd, thank You for never giving up
Your search for me when I am far from You. Amen.*

Hero

Remember not the former things,
nor consider the things of old.

ISAIAH 43:18 ESV

I had seen the man wearing the tattered coat and oversized ski cap around town on numerous occasions. He pulled a rusted child's wagon loaded with, what I guessed, were his earthly possessions. A yellow Labrador retriever followed him wherever he went.

Many times I ran across the pair at the library. The dog's leash was tied to a rail, and he seemed content to wait for his master's return. A bowl of water sat under the tree within the dog's reach. The man always sat at the same table off to the side of the main reading area. I assumed he used the library as a place to escape the seasonal weather.

I found out the man and his dog lived at a homeless shelter where he worked for meager wages. I was relieved to hear that he had a safe place to live. My friend also told me their names, Tim and Hero. Hero had once been a service dog who had saved his disabled master from a fire, which earned him his name. When his first master died, Hero came to live with Tim. I prayed for them whenever our paths crossed. I also left money at the shelter for the dog's upkeep after I was assured the man's basic needs were being met.

While visiting the library one afternoon, I asked where Tim and Hero were. The librarian told me a robbery had occurred on a side street, which connected the shelter and the library. An elderly lady had been the victim of a purse snatching, and Hero had wrestled the thief to the ground. The thief had hit Hero with an iron pipe and broken the dog's jaw. As the story spread, people donated money for Hero's veterinary care.

After Tim and Hero's episode with the purse thief, people saw Tim differently. Word spread that Tim was educated and had held a high company position before his life took a downward spiral. After losing his job, his marriage deteriorated. Tim fell into despair and ended up on the street. When Tim and Hero risked their lives to help the lady who was attacked their lives were changed. Tim now runs the homeless shelter. He and Hero, now recovered, visit schools and nursing homes as an outreach ministry.

All Tim and Hero needed was a second chance. Don't we all need a second chance? Just like them, if we bring our failures, painful memories, or poor choices to Jesus, He will grant forgiveness, direct our feet toward different paths, and fill our hearts with hope and purpose. God's grace and Jesus's gift of salvation means that whatever was in our past is wiped away and we can start each day anew.

Father, thank You for being a God of second chances,
for offering Your people restoration and grace. Amen.

In Agreement
With God

Praise be to the LORD forever! Amen and Amen.

PSALM 89:52 NIV

At four years old, you might think Bear, our chocolate Labrador-American Pit Terrier, would be in total agreement with our commands by now. You might think he would be obedient in everything we ask him to do: Come when he's called. Stay when he's told to stay. Give us a hardy "Amen, so be it. I'm in complete agreement with your requests," whenever we tell Bear to do something.

You might think that, but if you did, you would be wrong.

Just like many of us, Bear is inconsistent in his obedience and willingness to say amen to what we ask. Some days, he does great following directions. Other days, not so much, and I wonder what happened.

There are days when Bear is so sweet and does what I ask that I begin to think, *Yes! he's figured this all out!* only to have him do the exact opposite the next day when I give him a command.

I attribute Bear's lack of complete obedience to multiple factors, one being the fact that Bear truly is smart and, to his way of thinking, sees little wisdom in agreeing to all of our requests. I wish Bear would trust that my husband and I have Bear's best interest in mind and be obedient when we tell him to do something—or tell him not to do something.

But I wonder. Am I ever like Bear? Do I pick and choose

the things I'm in agreement with when God gives me a command even though I know He has my best interest in mind?

Sometimes my life moves along smoothly and it is easy to say amen to where God places me, what He gives me to do, and where He directs me to go.

But then there are days I plunge into sorrow, feeling defeated and discouraged. Say amen to this? You've got to be kidding. God is still in control, yes, but at times like these I may not be in complete and strong agreement with what is happening.

I keep hoping for the day Bear is in total agreement with what we tell him. I long for the day he says "so be it" to our requests. We do know what's best for him, after all. Do you think God hopes the same for us? Perhaps God hopes that no matter the situation one day I will state with every fiber of my being, "Amen. So be it! I'm in total agreement to Your plan, Lord. Your will be done, and do it through me."

Father, I long to follow Your will and be in strong agreement with it, but sometimes doing so seems difficult to accomplish. Help me embrace Your will in my life with a hardy, "Amen!"

Precious Little Things

*The generous will prosper; those who refresh others
will themselves be refreshed.*

PROVERBS 11:25 NLT

When Precious's owner died, the petite Pomeranian needed a home. Bob, the administrator, at the assisted-living facility where my Granny-Ma lived, brought the dog in, kindly explaining that Precious belonged to all the residents. But, when the dog took a special liking by Granny-Ma, Bob said she would be Precious's primary caretaker since Precious had "chosen" her.

Needless to say, Precious's presence brightened up every occasion. Old faces crinkled with delight when she pranced down the carpeted hallway toward a gathering. She instinctively knew how to skitter out of the path of walkers and wheelchairs and leap into the laps of those who needed a dose of joy. After an event, Precious ran so fast back "home" to Granny-Ma's room, it was hard to keep her in sight. However, she could be still and quiet when necessary. Once she spent an entire day sitting at the feet of the neighbor across the hall whose husband had just passed away. Precious had never voluntarily gone into that room before. Yet, somehow she sensed she was needed and offered the comfort of her presence as a soothing gift.

Most of the time, though, Precious perched on the arm of the recliner where my brother Phillip sat when he visited Granny-Ma. Now and then she would hop to the top of the chair and traipse across his broad shoulders, giving a gentle massage. She loved riding in the car with her "big brother" and would flatten herself out like a fluffy throw rug on the console beside his elbow.

Rebecca, my sister and a fashion diva, delighted in dressing Precious for every holiday season. Though this little darling was already adorable, she became doubly so when Rebecca took charge of her wardrobe. The residents really noticed her then and constantly beckoned her to come visit so they could examine her finery up close. Precious patiently complied.

In countless ways, Precious eased the ache of lonely hearts and brought a sparkle of delight to dreary days. This "little thing" proved that "little things" in life often offer the most joy.

What little things can we do to brighten someone's day? A cup of hot tea and a bit of friendly conversation. Maybe saying a pray with someone who seems lonely or stressed, or sharing a favorite scripture or passage from a book. Pick some flowers and arrange them in a vase to brighten up someone's room. Offer a shoulder rub or a hand massage to ease an arthritic ache. Creative and simple kindnesses. Like Precious, the kindnesses sent out come boomeranging back to the giver.

Father, today may we delight in giving and receiving precious tokens of Your love. Amen.

Love Drives Out
Fear

*There is no fear in love. But perfect love drives out fear,
because fear has to do with punishment.
The one who fears is not made perfect in love.*

1 JOHN 4:18 NIV

I first saw Summer online while browsing pictures of shelter dogs. She was a beautiful black Lab mix. The picture was taken at Halloween, and the shelter staff had put a bright orange frilly collar on her. She looked like she was smiling.

We visited the shelter to meet Summer and on the way home, the kids and I picked out a new dog bed, collar and leash, and a squeaky rubber chicken. Then we brought her home, looking forward to Summer becoming part of our family. However, I soon realized we had a problem: Summer was afraid to come in the house.

Summer had lived all her life at the shelter and had never been socialized to a home. She wasn't sure what to think about carpet. The washer and dryer made scary noises. She was particularly afraid to go through doors. She loved the attention we gave her, but she wouldn't come in unless I picked up the fifty-pound dog and carried her inside. When she did come in, she glued herself to my chair and trembled. We were ready to welcome Summer and make her part of our family, but fear took away her freedom to enjoy it.

I told the children we would have to be patient with her. We spent time in the yard every day, gently coaxing her closer to the door with bits of hot dogs and cooked chicken. When she did come in, I made sure to give her extra treats and reward her with lots of petting. Slowly she became more willing to come in. Then one night, Summer came in and put her paws up on the chair where I was sitting. I scratched her ears and petted her. She inched her way further into the chair until she was lying in my lap, tongue hanging out and looking pleased with herself. That's when I knew it was going to be okay. Summer was home.

Our experience with Summer made me wonder how often fear keeps me from freedom. Sometimes, like Summer, I stand outside, afraid to walk in and enjoy the freedom and blessings of a relationship with God. Often, moving forward into God's blessings can mean going through a door that looks a little scary. That door might be called "risk," or "change," or "out of my comfort zone."

Just as Summer's growing understanding of our love gave her confidence to come inside, my growing trust in God's love can give me courage to move forward into all the blessings He has for me. When we understand how much God loves us, it gives us the courage to face our fears. Love conquers fear.

Lord, when the future looks scary, may my confidence in Your love drive out all my fear. Amen.

Appreciating Nature

How many are your works, LORD!
In wisdom you made them all;
the earth is full of your creatures.

PSALM 104:24 NIV

Hank, a black Labrador, joined our family when he was eight weeks old. My husband and I thought our children might learn responsibility by caring for a pet. I wonder how we could have imagined they had time to do this as their schedules included school, soccer, gymnastics, and more.

Although my kids loved Hank, they didn't have time to properly care for him. Feeding and walking our patient boy fell to me, but it became a labor of love, not a chore. It was here I rediscovered something I'd lost—time alone in the woods with God. Now I had our gentle Labrador for companionship.

Each day, my faithful friend greeted me with a stretch and a tail wag. On the walking trail, Hank investigated everything with curiosity and enthusiasm. His ability to notice and appreciate all of God's creation opened my eyes to the tiniest of the marvels throughout the forest that I would have missed had it not been for Hank's attention. I remember the first time I spotted him looking down inside the whorl of a young corn plant. He stood with feet braced, nose down, and tail pointing. I moved in close to see what had captured his attention and discovered a line of lady bugs traveling up the spiral.

Hank often flushed coveys of quail, and sometimes we spied whitetail deer grazing in the clover. Songbirds always serenaded our afternoon adventures, but I learned to avoid the wild turkey roosts because Hank loved to roll in the fetid droppings.

Once, he stood and stared up into a tree full of crows, listening to their cacophony of caws as they scolded a barred owl. Hank gave a rare woof at the base of the tree as if to assist the fussing birds. Through the years, he treed raccoons and scampering chipmunks, but he never harmed anything.

On our walks, we'd stop at the creek and Hank would sit by my side while I told him and God about my day. Sitting by the stream, with water cascading over rocks, I was refreshed and renewed.

God gives humans the responsibility to care for His awe-inspiring world, and it was by watching my curious dog explore that I began to fully appreciate all the creatures this job entails. There are tiny living beings everywhere if you open your eyes and look. Heaven is here on earth. We just have to slow down and experience it with all our senses—and Hank showed me best how do that.

*Thank You, Father for Your glorious world
and for sending me a loyal companion to teach me
how to discover heaven on earth. Amen.*

Polly's Touch

When times get bad, people cry out for help. They cry for relief from being kicked around, but never give God a thought when things go well, when God puts spontaneous songs in their hearts, when God sets out the entire creation as a science classroom, using birds and beasts to teach wisdom.

JOB 35:9–11 MSG

Polly, a white German shepherd, was a trembling ball of fluff when she first bonded with my father. From the first, she seldom left his side, and after she grew into a tall and lanky youngster, she'd romp next to him in the garden or go for rides with him in his pickup.

But their companionship ran deeper than mere friendship. Prone to depression, my father would sink into deep, dark moods marked by silence and withdrawal. Polly would gently push her way through them, nudging him with her head until he stroked her, an action that lifted his mood and encouraged him to interact.

Polly's sensitivity to others, however, wasn't limited to my dad. When my daughter Rachel, who was severely disabled, visited my parents, Polly approached her with gentle caution. When Rachel would fuss, Polly would lay her head on Rachel's tummy, offering comfort, warmth, and reassurance. Rachel would settle immediately, batting her hands into Polly's neck and gripping her fur.

We'd put Rachel in the porch swing and Polly would linger near, bumping the swing anytime it slowed. If a stranger approached, she'd give a low growl of warning. No one was going to harm Rachel on her watch.

As Polly aged, my father got the opportunity to repay the compassion and empathy Polly had shown all of us. She still loved to ride in the truck, but arthritis in her hips meant she couldn't get in by herself. My father would lift her into the seat, and she'd take the trip proudly, her head held up, watching all that went by.

When lightning struck a field near their house, Polly felt the hit, and she became so mortally terrified of storms, she was a danger to herself. My father would sit on the floor, holding Polly tightly in his arms until it passed. Only with his touch would she calm.

The lessons we learned from this intelligent, perceptive animal seemed unending. She taught us the ultimate value that compassion, empathy, and understanding have in the lives of others. We saw the healing nature of a simple touch, and how reassurance can be offered to another just by being there.

Scripture often reminds us that God's presence is in all His creation. We just need to take a moment to look and listen and learn from what He has set before us. The world is our classroom, and the lessons go on forever when we remember to praise Him in all things, in good times as well as in the trials. He is always there.

Lord, help me see the wisdom You have put before me.
Let me learn from Your creation as well as Your Word. Amen.

A Love We
Can't Escape

I can never escape from your spirit!
I can never get away from your presence!

PSALM 139:7 NLT

Mom knew that a sure way to find a healthy dog was to choose the most energetic dog in the litter. As we gazed over the gate at the puppies available for adoption, one stood out. A teacup Yorkshire Terrier had backed a much larger Bichon Frisé into a corner. She certainly exhibited spunk. We took her home that afternoon.

A cap of golden hair accented the sleek black fur covering her body. She looked like a miniature chocolate cake with delicious yellow frosting. Since she was about the size of a giant muffin, her name seemed obvious to any baked goods lover. We'd call her "Cupcake."

Soon, all of our neighbors would also know Cupcake by name. How? Because all that vigor she exhibited at the breeder's was indicative of things to come. Cupcake was a runner. Perfecting the art of the fast break, she darted outside with the slightest crack of the door. Then, she'd run down the street like a wild animal on a quest for freedom.

With all the speed a ten-year-old girl could muster, I'd chase her down the road yelling, "Cupcake! Stop! Cupcake!" Soon, my mom and little brother would join in the chase. Often it required at least three family members to pin Cupcake in front of a neighbor's garage, snatch up her tiny body, and carry her back home.

This scenario repeated itself. For years. Although we worked to train Cupcake not to run away, she never let a chance to escape pass her by. One false click of the leash meant we'd be sprinting down that street again, yelling, "Cupcake! Cupcake! Cupcake!" the entire way. My adrenaline would race as I followed her around the block. But, I'd keep running. I adored that puppy. Not pursuing her was not an option.

Sometimes I fearfully shouted her name, praying she'd stay safe from passing cars or neighbors' aggressive dogs. Other times I desperately yelled for her, not knowing how much longer I could run. I worried that we'd never get her home. But no matter how far she strayed, I kept chasing.

Isn't that how God pursues us? There've been times when I decided my way was best. I found the crack in the door and escaped down my own path. I felt the warning from the Holy Spirit but foolishly decided to ignore it and rush toward the danger.

But, instead of leaving me alone to wander, God gently calls me back. In my heart I hear him repeat my name, beckoning me home. No matter how many times I stray, the Good Shepherd faithfully calls me back to His safety. He never gives up on me.

Lord, help me to surrender to Your ways
and show me that there's no place
I can go that is outside of Your reach. Amen.

Learning to See
in the Dark

For all who are led by the Spirit of God are children of God.

ROMANS 8:14 NLT

Liz will never forget the day she walked her son Logan to the bus stop. Halfway there, Logan suddenly turned around, smiled, and waved goodbye. "I didn't know that that was going to be the last time I saw his face," Liz said.

That morning a terrible headache forced Liz to lie down and rest, but when she woke up, the room had gone dark. She strained her eyes to see bits of light, but they faded into darkness. Liz went straight to the hospital where tests revealed that her sudden loss of sight would be permanent.

The world around Liz wasn't the only darkness she faced. Gloom shrouded her emotions. She had no idea how she could cope with the loss of her sight. As a single mom, Liz now faced the job of raising Logan blind alone *and* blind.

The devastating news sent her swirling into fear. Anxiety seized her at every turn. Simple tasks, like cooking and using a knife, easily overwhelmed her. The thought of crossing the street by herself terrified Liz.

But then, God's grace came into her life in an unexpected form. "I thought my life was over, and then I got Brice," Liz said. Comfort and relief showed up as a very special Golden Retriever.

Brice, her assigned guide dog, helped Liz realize that her life wasn't over, that she had so much to live for. With Brice's help, Liz learned to travel safely, avoid obstacles, and navigate crowds. The Golden Retriever, trained to stop at curbs and stairs, helped her regain much of her mobility and confidence.

Her bond with Brice runs much deeper. "Little did I know he would become a part of me."

Her guide dog seemed to sense when Liz was having a bad day. Drawing near, he would jump up on the couch with her for a cuddle. With Brice's help, Liz has been able to overcome both the physical and emotional obstacles of blindness.

Just as Brice comforted Liz, the Holy Spirit longs to comfort us in our own seasons of darkness. He wants to guide us through any obstacles we might face and help us navigate through all of life's joys, struggles, and moments in between. When we're confused by which choice to make, God's Spirit is waiting to lead us. He wants to be our guide. We must cling to the Lord, training our ears to listen and our hearts to follow His nudges. When we learn to follow His lead, and not our own understanding, we learn what it means to "walk by faith, not by sight" (2 Corinthians 5:7 NASB).

Lord Jesus, I long to hear and follow Your Spirit;
help me today to live in obedience to You. Amen.

Scruffy's Choice

See what great love the Father has lavished on us,
that we should be called children of God!

1 JOHN 3:1 NIV

"Dad, can we have one of the puppies?" Our sons discovered that Scruffy, the neighborhood dog, had delivered puppies under their shed. We had always told the boys they could get a dog when they were old enough, mostly as a way to skirt the issue, but now they saw their chance.

"We'll see when they're ready, but, for now, they have to stay with their mommy."

Scruffy roamed the neighborhood each day, stopping for food and attention at each house. She was such a good-natured dog that no one turned her down, and she was well known in the area. Her appearance matched her name as her fuzzy, shaggy hair stuck out around her small body. She appeared to be a Yorkie mix, or a "Heinz 57" as we say in Kentucky.

The weeks passed, and our sons grew impatient. "Dad, we want that puppy! Someone else is going to take it if we don't get it!" They had chosen a favorite, a shaggy girl much like Scruffy. We were not sure they were ready for the responsibility, so I tried to delay a bit longer. "When they're ready, we'll try to get that one."

At around the six week mark, when the pups were ready for weaning, my wife and I were relaxing on our porch as the boys played. In the distance we spotted Scruffy coming our way with something in her mouth. Upon closer look, we realized it was the pup my boys had picked out. Scruffy came up on the porch, dropped the pup at my feet, and walked back across the road.

How could we argue with that? Our boys squealed with delight as their wish for a dog had finally come true. My wife and I agreed that it was meant to be, and we decided to name the puppy "Cleo." Thirteen years later, she is still part of our family. Even though my sons have moved on to college, Cleo still brings us joy and is my walking buddy.

Has someone ever entered your life at just the right time? Maybe you prayed for a friend, a mate, or even a child, and God answered that prayer seemingly "out of the blue," possibly in an unexpected way. Our sons had hoped and prayed for a dog for quite a while, but God provided one in His way and in His timing. In the end, Scruffy chose us to adopt her baby, and this action was a lovely example of how God trusts us with our loved ones and places them in our lives at the right time.

Father, thank You for bringing special people into our lives,
and give me faith to trust You
and Your timing when I need someone. Amen.

Stay Alert

Stay alert! Watch out for your great enemy, the devil.
He prowls around like a roaring lion,
looking for someone to devour.

1 PETER 5:8 NLT

We have a nightly visitor—an opossum—and our dog, Bear, is not happy about it. I don't know where Mr. Possum goes during the day, but our chocolate Labrador-American Pit Terrier believes it is his responsibility to deter the intruder during the night. It's bad enough for our poor dog to put up with the cat from across the street who spends his evenings curled up on our front porch chair. But the backyard is Bear Territory. No varmints allowed.

Bear takes this intrusion into his yard seriously. Many a morning, he wakes up at 2:30 a.m. to sniff out violators of his space and secure the perimeter. I have no idea why Bear believes this is the prime time for possum chasing, but I know my husband wishes Bear didn't wake him up to make his rounds through the backyard.

As I pondered Bear's vigilance against things that intrude and threaten our yard, I wondered how well we stay on guard against those things that go bump in the night during the course of our lives. Do we stay alert against spiritual attacks that the devil hurls our way, which can come out of nowhere and catch us with our defenses down? Are we mindful of the things that by themselves might seem innocent, but if allowed to become habits can lead us down paths we should not follow?

How about the times we rationalize our behavior, knowing it really isn't right?

We may eat lunch with a coworker of the opposite sex more often than we should. After all, they understand us when our spouse doesn't, so what's the harm in that? We may watch shows and movies or read books and magazines that would make our grandmother blush. We need to stay current with the trends, right? We may lose our temper, become angry, and spew harmful words that we can't take back. Can we help it if we have a short fuse? We may decide it won't hurt to skip church today, or next week, or the week after that. We can worship God anywhere, can't we?

These are some things that may go bump in the night as we go through life, and if we aren't careful to guard against them, they could take up residence and be doubly hard to remove. Just as Bear is vigilant to protect our perimeters from intruders, we need to be watchful against spiritual intruders that threaten to undo us. The Bible tells us how. Reading God's Word is like using a guidebook to life, with wise instructions and hearty encouragement for each day.

Father, when the enemy prowls around looking for someone
to devour, keep me vigilant and alert with my eyes open
to the things that pull me away from You,
and protect me with Your power. Amen.

Beauty Shop Convert

Anyone who belongs to Christ has become a new person.
The old life is gone; a new life has begun!

2 CORINTHIANS 5:17 NLT

I am always renewed after a relaxing day at the spa. Unbelievably, Maggie is too. How she arrived in my neighborhood of small farms remains a mystery, but this Pyrenees-Old English sheepdog mix was hardly obscure. As a pup, she reached nearly one hundred pounds and became ironically known as The Big White Dog. Within just a few months, her white coat showed a pink-brown tinge from the Tennessee earth with the cockle burrs and imbedded sticks, hay, and leaves, giving her the appearance of a walking garbage can.

Her odiferous persona was overridden by a sweet, affectionate nature. Sadly, she disappeared for a while but re-emerged weeks later even more filthy and emaciated. The renter on a nearby farm who cared for the dog had moved out, leaving Maggie without a home base and regular meals.

There was only one choice for me. She succumbed to capture through a good meal during which I explained conditions for surrender. My veterinarian was confident adoption of an abandoned, neglected dog would not invoke any legal repercussions. At the shampoo tub two technicians groaned as Maggie waited for a bath and haircut.

Two spoiled Pooches already occupied spots in my home and another face at the food bowl could get ugly. Would Maggie be able to transition from vagabond to pampered pup?

My prayers were answered when I witnessed the reaction she received when we arrived home.

Sporting what became her signature cut—a cross between a sheared Poodle puppy and a Chinese Crested—she approached her housemates and, after a few sniffs, they relaxed together, Maggie enjoying her first real bed. After that I scheduled my spa days to coincide with hers and we both returned home happy and refreshed.

Even though the Pyrenees breed was queen of the field, Maggie adapted to inside living with finesse. She benefited from the companionship of a snuggling cat in her mammoth dog bed. Regular food and snacks convinced the weary traveler to give up the struggle and yield to loving hands that never failed her.

I've often wondered what could have happened to her had I not intervened. Her inherent beauty never would have emerged, and true contentment of a fulfilled, safe, and healthy life would sadly have been missed. Submission to my conditions had saved her life.

The Savior is always on the lookout for disheveled, hopeless travelers, seeing beyond their present condition to a fruitful life with a fresh chance. The Groomer washes away the old dirt, offering an opportunity to emerge afresh, and then places us in the family of God, a welcome space complete with nourishment and new friends for life.

Lord, when I've wandered, clean me up,
take me home, and make me new. Amen.

A New Normal

Whatever is good and perfect is a gift coming down to us from God our Father, who created all the lights in the heavens.

JAMES 1:17 NLT

For more than twenty-five years, my father worked at a job he disliked with only one goal in mind—to get my brother and me through college. He had never finished high school so his options were always limited. He started driving a logging truck in 1942 when he was sixteen to help with the family expenses.

He enjoyed being an independent trucker, and he relished the time it gave him to indulge in his true love: carpentry. However, when the family finances went topsy-turvy, he signed on with a major trucking firm for the security. He despised the restrictions and the trucks, which eventually took a toll on his health. But he persevered, determined that his kids would have the education he never did.

My brother went all the way to a doctorate. I received a master's degree. Then, his goal completed, my father sank into a depression dark enough that the entire family became frightened for him. Working at a job he hated, his age, his failing health, and his limited family time all crashed in on him. We tried everything to revive him but nothing worked, until Polly.

As a child, my father had a dream about a white German Shepherd, a dream so powerful that it stayed with him and he'd always longed for such a dog. But with a limited income, he never saw a reason to buy an expensive purebred when so many others needed homes. And he always had dogs around.

After a lot of prayer—and a long discussion with my mother—my husband and I bought him the dog of his dreams. The change in him was immediate. The white ball of fluff became his constant companion. We encouraged him to retire. Once he did he began to thrive as he expanded his garden and took up carpentry again.

With Polly at his side, my father found his new normal. When he had his first heart attack, she was as attentive as a nurse, lying by the couch within petting range. Then, as his health began to falter again, we worried what would happen to Polly if he died. But Polly went first, after only nine years. My father grieved, but he too was ill, and he passed away a few months later.

Polly was the light in my father's life that shattered an overwhelming darkness. And, examining the circumstances that brought her into our lives, I believe God had planned from the time my father was a boy to bring Polly to us, a gift that would lift my father in his last years and keep him focused on the positive.

Lord, I know that everything good in my life
is a gift from You—may I always remember
Your goodness and Your gifts to me. Amen.

Adoring the Master

Shout for joy to the Lord, all the earth.
Worship the Lord with gladness;
come before him with joyful songs.

PSALM 100:1-2 NIV

Whenever I come home—whether I've been gone only a few minutes on an errand or several days teaching at a conference—my Dachshund, Mollie Mae, greets me with the same over-the-top enthusiasm. She starts by jumping up on my legs and grinning at me. Yes, my dog grins. She shows her teeth and actually smiles at me. Then as I say, "You're such a good girl. I missed you so much, Mollie Mae," she goes into her vocal display of affection. She cocks her head back and begins howling in celebration of my homecoming. Finally, as I reach down to pet her, she rolls over on her back so I can rub her belly. She's also letting me know that she is in total submission to me by lying in such a vulnerable position. She absolutely adores me and she is passionate about showing her love. I bet your dog greets you with that same adoration.

We can learn much from our dogs. They have given us a perfect example to follow when coming into the presence of their master. They show enthusiasm, adoration, submission and honor. Do we do the same when we enter into the presence of our Master? Do we run into His presence, worship Him and sing our praises? Sadly, I don't think I show that same enthusiasm when I squeeze in a few minutes for my quiet time with God each day. Many times I'm so rushed and busy with the day that I barely give Him any attention at all.

Maybe you've also felt guilty of this same nonchalant attitude toward spending time with God. But we can remedy that. We can begin anew this very day and praise Him with all of our might! We can get excited about the fact that we have access to Almighty God any time of the day, and that He wants to spend time with us. How awesome is that!

You don't have to howl at heaven to show your adoration. Even if you can't sing a note, you can worship the Master in your own way. He won't even care if you sing off key. And, you don't have to hit your knees to pray, but once in a while I find that I do my best praying when I physically bow low before the Lord. All you have to do is take the time to get into His presence and love on Him and let Him love on you. Like the Word says, "Enter into His gates with thanksgiving, and into His courts with praise" (Psalm 100:4 NKJV). You'll come away feeling refreshed, renewed and truly loved.

Father, help me take time to praise You
and give You the honor You so deserve. Amen.

Calming the Storm

He stilled the storm to a whisper;
the waves of the sea were hushed.

PSALM 107: 29 NIV

Few things have terrified me more than witnessing Adam, my autistic seven-year-old neighbor, endure a meltdown in the grocery store. When this little boy experiences sensory overload, it leads to a complete loss of self-control.

Adam's mom didn't know what to do, but then she read several articles about service dogs assisting children like him, and she started searching for a specially trained canine. Months later, as Adam's name sat on waiting lists, she asked her friends to pray for a dog for him. God answered and sent Bailey, a Golden Retriever-Lab mix.

As his protector, Bailey would be tethered to Adam and prevent him from leaving the house and bolting into the street. The gentle dog would become an anchor and help keep Adam focused in this world instead of disappearing into his own.

Sleeping a full night without a disturbance was an anomaly before Bailey joined the home. Afterward, if Adam woke up during the night, the calming presence of this pooch soothed him back to sleep. His parents also rested more peacefully knowing that Bailey watched over their son, and that her barking will awaken them if Adam left his bedroom.

Caretakers learned to watch the dog for clues about Adam's level of anxiety. If Bailey started to lick her boy, it was an alert that he might need to be removed from a situation and the dreaded meltdown could be avoided. Bailey would crawl into Adam's lap, providing the same comfort of a heavy warm blanket. My friend tells me more than one crisis had been averted by the dog's attention and actions. Bailey has never been known to lose patience with Adam, even when his behavior is unacceptable to others. Adam rarely speaks, but sometimes he talks to Bailey who listens without condemnation.

Adam's challenges are different than the norm, but we all have the same needs. Do you want a best friend who will listen to your problems without judgment? Jesus is patiently waiting with open arms. If you've wandered from Him, don't despair, because nothing can separate you from His tether. When a tempest brews, you too have an anchor, just like Bailey's hold on Adam. If you awaken in the night, know there is nothing to fear with Jesus as your protector because He's watching over you. He will wrap His arms around you, and it's more comforting than a warm blanket. He can calm any storm and fill you with a peace that surpasses all understanding.

Sometimes, waiting for an answer can be difficult, but trust God and His plan. Bailey, the perfect dog for Adam, was worth the wait. Call on Jesus and trust Him. He knows exactly what you need.

Father, thank You for sending me exactly what I need.
I know I can trust You to calm every storm and fill me
with a peace that surpasses all understanding. Amen.

The Golden Rule

*So in everything, do to others what you would have them
do to you, for this sums up the Law and the Prophets.*

MATTHEW 7:12 NIV

"If that dog's here tomorrow, I'm going to shoot it," the grouchy homeowner said as he pointed to the stray red dog running across his property.

"What if I lock her in the barn and take her home when I leave at the end of the day?" My husband was painting his farm house and hated to see an innocent dog shot. The homeowner agreed.

We welcomed the stray into our apartment so we could find her owners. She appeared to be a purebred Irish Setter. Surely, she'd only wandered from home. But no one ever stepped forward to claim her. Why? We found out a couple months later.

Her first trip to the vet revealed Lady, as we called her, had heart worms. I was devastated. You see, even though she was only about two years old and would survive the treatment fairly well, we'd have to scrimp and save to come up with two hundred dollars for the medication. I left the vet brokenhearted as I crunched the numbers. Since we were newly married, every penny earned was earmarked for a bill. How could we afford such an expensive treatment?

Then I looked at her proudly sitting tall on the passenger seat—like a royal, redheaded princess who deserved to live a long life. If I was her, I'd want someone to take a chance on me. Tears flowed. My heart had won the battle. We paid a couple of bills late and sacrificed our usual dinner by eating sandwiches for awhile, but this way she got the treatment she needed immediately.

Now I'm not completely sure if Jesus meant for the "others" in the Golden Rule to include animals or not, but I'd like to think so. After all, the first two chapters in Genesis tell of the creation and care of animals, the Sabbath included rest for the work animals (Deuteronomy 5:14), and when God sent the flood, He saved two of every kind (Genesis 7:2–3). He sent ravens to feed Elijah (1 Kings 17:4–6), provided a great fish to teach Jonah a lesson (Jonah 1:17), and opened the mouth of Baalam's donkey to set the record straight (Numbers 22: 21–33). Jesus also used animals when teaching parables, including, "Are not two sparrows sold for a penny? Yet not one of them will fall to the ground outside your Father's care" (Matthew 10:29 NIV).

From a matted up stray to a beloved family pet, Lady lived a long, happy life. I'd have to say that following the Golden Rule has had its benefits. Doing what's best for others usually turns out to be what's best for us.

Thank you, Lord, for sharing Your tender heart with us
and giving us a tender heart for others,
whether two-legged or four. Amen.

It Seemed Like
the Right Thing

For I do not do the good I want to do,
but the evil I do not want to do—this I keep on doing.

ROMANS 7:19 NIV

David parked his mail truck in the driveway, retrieved the package he needed to deliver, and walked to the front door. He knocked loudly so the homeowner would hear him and then he took a startled step backward as a white blur ran toward him and jumped on the screen door, popping it open.

The door swung wide and a knee-high white blur zoomed by him. And then David took another startled step backward as—without a word—a woman ran out the door in pursuit. He thought the white blur was a Poodle, but everything happened so fast that he didn't even get a good look. He stood there in shock watching the homeowner chase the dog down the street.

David considered helping her chase the Poodle, but some bad experiences with dogs while delivering the mail had left him leery about running after one.

He needed a signature for the package so he decided to sit on the porch until the woman caught her dog and came home. That sounded like a good idea until long minutes ticked by. He waited, and waited, and waited, but she didn't come back. Just as he decided he'd better get back on his route again, he noticed a white Poodle walking down the street toward him—but the woman was nowhere in sight.

The dog seemed friendly. Her tail was wagging and she acted like she wanted to play. David looked down the street for the homeowner, and when he didn't see her, he picked the Poodle up, opened the screen door, and put the pooch inside. At least the woman would be relieved when she got home and found her dog was safe.

He got back into his mail truck, backed out of the driveway, and headed down the street in the opposite direction. But just as he got to the corner where he would have to turn, he noticed something in his rear view mirror. The homeowner walked back into her yard. And that's when David realized there might be a problem. A really big furry problem—because she was carrying a white Poodle—which meant that the one he'd put inside her house wasn't her dog!

I laughed at David's story when I heard it, but then I realized that I often do the same thing spiritually. I mean to do well. I really do. But then I neglect to ask God for direction. I move out under my own steam, thinking I am wise. And then I mess up, doing exactly the opposite of what I intended to do.

That's where time in His Word proves invaluable. And that's when time in prayer enables me to hear those important instructions from Him.

Father, help me to listen to You
before I take even one step. Amen.

Stand Your Ground

Though an army encamp against me,
my heart shall not fear; though war may rise against me,
in this I will be confident.

PSALM 27:3 NKJV

Crimson was twenty pounds of confidence. A silver-gray Cockapoo, she showed off her alpha tendencies anytime the opportunity arose, which sometimes put her in conflict with her human companions, cats, other dogs, the vet, and her doggy day care owner. But she would stand her ground with all comers. She commanded any dog in the vicinity, and did so without a snarl or a growl. She took over with her presence and her attitude.

The owner of her doggy day care had never seen anything like it. "She doesn't nip or bark. She just strikes a pose and the rest gather around." In the play area, dogs of a similar size would lurk near her, and if she sat down to rest, they would form a circle around her. When a visiting dog to the day care once tried to take the alpha status, the other dogs put him in his place. Crimson never had to move a muscle.

The only time when Crimson would take action was if another dog tried to get between her and her owner, a woman with whom she had an extraordinary bond. Jealous of even a vocal greeting to another animal, Crimson reacted with snarls and snaps if her owner tried to caress the intruder. The two of them were a pack, and no interlopers were welcome.

Otherwise well behaved, Crimson's confidence became legendary in the neighborhood the day the local pit bull slipped his leash and charged her, barking ferociously. Both humans watched in terror as the two dogs came together. Crimson stood, legs braced and apart, head held high, tailed curled up over her back. The pit bull stopped a few inches away, announcing himself with a few more booming barks. Crimson stood silently.

After a moment, the pit bull hushed, and the two dogs stared at each other. Crimson sniffed. A second later, the pit bull whimpered and began to wag his tail. Crimson did the same, and they soon danced around each other with exploratory sniffing.

Like Crimson, we live in a world where the unexpected sometimes charges at us from all directions. We face trials that previous generations never dreamed of. The busyness of our lives can be overwhelming as dozen of obligations command our attention. Under such pommelling, we can be tempted to give in, compromising our principles and even our faith.

We need to remember that God is our strength, our refuge—even the source of our confidence. When He is with us, we can stand firm and face every challenge that comes our way.

Lord, forgive us our weaknesses, and help us remember that You can provide all the strength, wisdom, and confidence we need to face the world. All we have to do is ask. Amen.

Who Sets the Pace?

Show me Your ways, O LORD; teach me Your paths.

PSALM 25:4 NKJV

When our chocolate Labrador-American Pit Terrier, Bear, was a puppy, our walks were anything but pleasant. Calling them walks would be a stretch. They were more like tugs. I looked forward to the day Bear and I could take leisurely walks without me constantly needing to redirect his path and pace. The joyful day did arrive, but it wasn't without a lot of hard work.

In the beginning, after every two or three strides of our walk I had to repeat the same routine. I planted my feet, dug in my heels, and told Bear to sit. Bear sat and obediently looked up at me. Whenever we started to walk again, Bear took his first few step obediently in the heel position at my left side. After those first steps, however, I believe Bear must have said to himself, "Let's see how far I can tug her down the road before she makes me sit again."

By the time our walks ended, both my arms were tired from keeping a firm grip on the leash. I was exhausted, and realized without a doubt I was not César Millán, the Dog Whisperer.

Our walks would have been easier if I let Bear do whatever he wanted to do. I could have jogged behind Bear, and pretended I was actually the one in charge. But if I did, Bear would've always walked ahead of me instead of *with* me.

As I thought about Bear and his training, I thought that maybe I am more like Bear than I would like to admit. Sometimes my walk with God looks like my walks with Bear.

I head off down the path of my choosing and set the pace that suits me. I pay little attention, if any, to the path God sets before me or the pace He wants to travel. When I do that, it is as if I expect God to adjust to me instead of the other way around.

How many times do I race off ahead of God, confident I know where I am going, setting my own pace to get there, and giving little attention to God's direction? How many times has God had to plant His feet, refuse to budge, and wait for me to sit and look at Him before He leads me in the next steps of my life?

I can tug and pull against God's plan, pace, and path. That's called free will. Or I can submit to God's plan, pace, and path. When I do that, I get to walk *with* God. That's called freedom in Christ.

Father, I know there are times I strike out on my own,
expecting You to follow along beside me instead of walking
with You at the pace and the direction You set.
Teach me to follow where You lead. Amen.

Becoming Family

The LORD keeps you from all harm and watches over your life.
The LORD keeps watch over you
as you come and go, both now and forever.

PSALM 121:7-8 NLT

For Jon and Jenna, their dog, Charlie, isn't just another member of the family. She helped them become a family. The East Coast couple received the Australian Shepherd puppy as a wedding present—with just one catch. They needed to fly to Oklahoma to pick her up. So, Jon and Jenna bought tickets and headed back to the red-dirt farming community where Jon grew up. When Jon met Charlie, it was love at first sight.

"They had an immediate connection, one that I have never seen before," Jenna said.

Perhaps the dog reminded Jon a little of himself. They both grew up on a farm, same red dirt under their nails. Both loved the outdoors. The puppy also had to make the long trip back to Massachusetts—the same journey Jon made the year before when he traded the community he loved for the woman he loved more.

The cross-country move, however, had left Jon lonely, and he struggled to make friends. When they brought Charlie home, she brought sunshine back into Jon's life.

"When Charlie became part of our family, I never saw that loneliness anymore," Jenna said. "I feel that God sent Jon his best friend."

Jon wasn't the only person who benefited from Charlie's presence in their home. Charlie taught Jenna patience and proved to her that she could someday tackle the demands of motherhood. Dealing with a high-strung puppy makes a baby look easy.

When Jenna became pregnant, Charlie's herding instinct kicked in. She became visibly more protective, especially of the mom-to-be. Once the nursery went up, Charlie moved her sleeping spot near the crib. When Ellie was born, Jon introduced the baby to Charlie and she stayed close to the baby throughout infancy. "Immediately she knew that this was her baby," Jenna said.

Like a sentry on duty, Charlie continues to keep a close watch over the family. The dog can't settle in for the night until she makes her rounds, checking each bedroom. Jenna and Jon watch the same scene unfold each day and can't escape how it reflects God's gentle protection.

Just like Charlie, God never lets down His guard when it comes to watching over His family. He sticks close to His children throughout every season of life, guiding us into the future. He isn't just the God of moments, but of lifetimes and generations. God even knows how to rewrite family histories with His love.

In Charlie, we catch a glimpse of God's much deeper loyalty—the loyalty of a Savior who gave up His own life so that we could live. Not only that, but through Jesus, God invites us into a forever family that never ends.

Jesus, help me recognize Your presence each day, and show me how Your fingerprints are seen throughout my entire life. Amen.

Our Safe Place

The LORD is my light and my salvation—whom shall I fear?
The LORD is the stronghold of my life—of whom shall I be afraid?

PSALM 27:1 NIV

Several years ago when my daughter finished college, she moved from a small, rural town to a large city with a high crime rate. My motherly instincts went on high alert, so my husband and I helped her find an apartment where safety measures were a priority.

A week later, we packed her belongings, loaded them into the car, and got her settled into her new living quarters. After helping to arrange furniture, scout out the closest grocery store, and determine the best route to her job, we cautioned her about safety. Every time we talked with Leslie, we ended the conversation with a blessing and a prayer for her safekeeping.

Six months after her move she telephoned us and told us a robber had broken into her apartment and stolen some items. Leslie was at work when the thief entered her home, but she was traumatized nonetheless.

Leslie's apartment had become a place of fear and unhappiness. She had trouble sleeping. Any unknown noise would cause her labored breathing. Even though better locks were installed and additional security measures were implemented at her apartment complex, Leslie's fear did not subside.

After learning pets were allowed in her building, Leslie decided to adopt a large dog that would provide a menacing presence. A coworker's family bred German Shepherds, and she offered to help Leslie purchase a dog that would help her feel safe. When we met the breeder, the puppy was on a leash. Leslie stopped short, surprised by the size of the black and tan puppy. The breeder then showed Leslie how to handle and bond with the dog, which she named Sheba. The immediate connection between human and animal was apparent as Leslie's tense demeanor dissolved under an onslaught of sweet puppy kisses.

Leslie began to feel safe with Sheba in the apartment. Noises in the night no longer caused Leslie to panic. She felt secure when she inserted the key into the lock on her apartment's door, knowing Sheba waited on the other side of it.

What a beautiful picture the psalmist's words give to those who are fearful. Fear comes in many forms and can rob a person of a fulfilled life. Just as Leslie felt safe in the presence of Sheba, so we can trust the Lord to be our shield and defender. We can live a life free from fear as we put our trust in Him. In this world, bad things will happen, but knowing that God goes before us and is our ever present help, especially in troubled times, we can rest assured because of His presence and love. All we have to do is seek Him out and our fear will be wiped away.

Father, thank You for being our protector
and place of safety. Amen.

Hearing His Voice

My sheep listen to my voice; I know them, and they follow me.
I give them eternal life, and they shall never perish;
no one will snatch them out of my hand.

JOHN 10:27–28 NIV

My uncle raised hunting dogs, and when our family went on vacation we would take our little Beagle-Dachshund mix to stay with him. The first time we took Blondie to his house, my uncle helped me get her settled in the pen before we went into the house for supper. After supper we went back out to feed the dogs. My uncle strolled along beside me, gently shaking a coffee can filled with dog food as he walked. As we approached the pen, my uncle's hunting dogs heard him coming. The pack of Foxhounds and coonhounds came running for the gate and sat at attention, eyes fixed on my uncle and the coffee can. But I didn't see Blondie. I finally found her down at the far end of the pen, tongue lolling out of her mouth and sitting back on her haunches with a curious look in her eyes.

After we returned from vacation it was a different story. My uncle and I walked out to the pen with the coffee can, and this time when all the dogs came running, Blondie was right there in the middle of them. During the week we had been gone, she had learned the sound of that coffee can rattling meant food. She had begun to learn my uncle's voice.

As believers in Christ, we learn to hear the voice of our Master. Recognizing someone's voice means you've spent enough time with that person to know the sound of their voice. In the same way, coming to recognize the voice of the

Lord is a sign of relationship. It means we've spent enough time with God to recognize His voice when He speaks. That means spending time in Bible study, worship, and prayer, and also spending time in obedience, even when it's hard. As we learn what God says and put it into practice, we build a relationship with God that helps us learn and respond to the sound of His voice.

The beauty of knowing God's voice is that it is not a one-sided relationship. If we know God's voice, He also knows ours. Just as a shepherd can tell his sheep apart by the shape of their heads and the patterns of their wool, God intimately knows us and desires us to follow Him. And God gives the most precious of all gifts to those who know Him and are known by Him: eternal life and the promise that no one can snatch us from His hand.

Today, spend time listening to the voice of your Master. Rejoice that you are known by Him and safe in His loving care.

Lord, help me recognize Your voice and obey.
Thank You for the security and safety
of being known by You. Amen.

Blue Ribbon Grace

Keep my commandments and live;
keep my teaching as the apple of your eye.

PROVERBS 7:2 ESV

My Airedale's failure in obedience training quickly became apparent in the company of other dogs. During group activities in the ring, Toby spent more effort investigating the dog in front of him than he did listening to me or the instructor. He learned the basic commands well and obediently performed at home before an audience of one. However, in the ring, instinctual Terrier curiosity and energy landed Toby at the bottom of his class of mellow, happy Golden Retrievers and laid-back hounds.

Because of our failure, I came to appreciate the intense effort of a handler and her dog. I block out two evenings each year to watch the Westminster Dog Show, accompanied by my two slightly odiferous Airedales sharing the sofa. The Terrier group shows in the final class and by then I've witnessed many teams parade around experienced judges.

Each animal is given one last chance to demonstrate its stuff when the judge commands, "One last time around, please." The judge steps out in front, serious and composed, bringing years of experience to the ring to celebrate and delight in each breed's finest expression and bloodlines. Love, not criticism, influences the decisions.

The handler brings out her brushes and combs, adjusts the leash, and offers a pat or kiss for inspiration prior to the final display. What goes on before approaching the judge doesn't influence the final judgment of the dog.

Because the judge knows the qualities of each breed, he knows what is required to achieve optimal performance. His evaluation begins when the dog steps out with the handler. Success in the ring is achieved not only by an obedient dog but by the acceptable, finished work of a capable handler.

I see the grace of God reflected in the judge, his position, and the stance he maintains. Like the primping done before approaching the judge, the Holy Spirit has had to primp and fluff many times to make me presentable. I've needed extra jerks on my chain to get my attention and I do well for an audience of one but become distracted by peers.

The relief I experience when my handler, my Lord and Savior, nods in my direction is not met with derision. The Judge offers love and acceptance as I demonstrate my efforts to become more Christ-like in my daily walk. When the Judge calls, I step out because I've been prepared by my Handler according to His standards. I follow and obey, knowing His work is already approved.

Toby never acquired a blue ribbon, only a certificate of participation. I loved him nonetheless as he continued to perform as a faithful companion. God extends the same grace to me; I'm accepted and loved because His Son is my Master.

Lord, may I always seek to keep Your commands
and rest in knowing it's not my performance
but Christ's work that makes me acceptable. Amen.

Blessings
in Disguise

This hope will not lead to disappointment.
For we know how dearly God loves us, because he has given us
the Holy Spirit to fill our hearts with his love.

ROMANS 5:5 NLT

Many years ago, my husband, Michael, was riding with his mom and brothers to the grocery store. She parked the car and he spotted the sign first: "Free Puppies." His short, six-year-old legs sprinted to the cardboard box and looked inside to discover six yapping Beagle-mix pups.

The last thing his mother needed was more responsibility. Her husband served in Vietnam and she had three active boys. After giving her crew a few minutes to examine and play with the litter, she gently pulled her sons into the store.

As they left the market, she surprised everyone when she paused in front of the crate where only two remained, and she lifted one out. The paws of this one seemed large, and he was twice the size of his brother. When she inhaled the soft milk breath of the puppy, her heart softened, and the resolve to leave without a dog dissolved. They left with both of the black and tan pups and named them Hamburger and Pickles, because that's what they'd visited the store to get.

Hamburger grew into those large feet, and it turns out Pickles was the perfect name for the runt. Consider the size of a pickle to a hamburger and it matched this pair of brothers. It turns out, three boys and two dogs are a perfect combination.

Those hounds followed and protected their youngsters through the woods on many adventures. My mother-in-law could always tell where her troop played by listening to the dogs howl. Those Beagles were constantly on alert as they watched over their charges.

Sometimes, God gives us unexpected gifts, but we have to be paying attention or we'll miss them. My mother-in-law lived by listening to her heart. Many would have seen those free puppies as another duty, a burden, and walked away empty handed. But Hamburger and Pickles blessed my husband's childhood home in countless ways, and those dogs taught them many lessons, such as loving and protecting their family, and being a loyal and true friend. I believe God created dogs for just this purpose, giving us a glimpse of His generous nature.

Hamburger and Pickles looked worthless to many and were rejected just as many missed the Messiah. God stepped down from His throne, lived among us for a while, and demonstrated His great love for us, but many rejected him. If only they had listened with their hearts they could have received the most precious blessing of all. May we all learn to listen with our heart and never miss God's blessings that are sometimes in disguise.

Father, help me to be alert to all Your blessings,
and to always listen to what You're saying in my heart. Amen.

Loyal Protection

Love . . . always protects, always trusts, always hopes, always perseveres. Love never fails.

1 CORINTHIANS 13:6-8 NIV

Cuddles had never bitten anyone, not in all her six years with Louise. She barked a lot, yes, normal for a seven-pound Peekapoo. She challenged squirrels, mail carriers, cats, and those strange folks who stole the garbage. She would bounce from window to table to door in alarm, her yips echoing through the house as her salt-and-pepper fur shivered and fluffed around her. But she'd never nipped at anyone.

Until Rachel came along. Rachel's disabilities meant that she couldn't walk or talk, but dogs of all kinds adored her, responding to her vulnerability with a guarded, protective spirit, Cuddles included. However, other dogs that adopted Rachel did so with a gentle kindness, whereas Cuddles was fierce.

From the moment Louise became one of Rachel's caregivers, Cuddles adhered herself to the eight-year-old's side. She would snuggle up against Rachel's back, her head resting on the child's hip. Her gaze followed everyone who came close, and if anyone approached, she'd give a low growl of warning.

Unfortunately for Cuddles, her size meant few people took her seriously. Despite strict instructions otherwise, the other children in the house found it amusing to tease Cuddles by "threatening" Rachel. They would pat her diaper, which would make Rachel giggle and Cuddles bark and snarl. They thought it was funny, right up to the day Cuddles's teeth latched on to an arm.

The young man was fourteen, old enough to know better, and when Cuddles nipped him, he was angry and frustrated. As Louise tended to the minor wound, the boy wanted to know why his own dog had bit him.

Louise smiled. "You need to look at her heart, not her size. Rachel is helpless, and Cuddles loves her. Love isn't just about hugs and kisses and snuggles. It's also about looking out for those we care for. Cuddles doesn't know you're teasing, that you're not really going to hurt Rachel, and she is going to protect those she loves. You should respect that. And you should also do the same." It was a lesson in love that he never forgot.

In today's culture, we're often surrounded by depictions of love that are anything but biblical and can be misleading. Instead, if we turn to Paul's "love chapter" (1 Corinthians 13), we'll find a description of love that is deep, all encompassing, and eternal. Love perseveres. And love protects.

Lord, I look to You for the true nature of love.
Help me remember that we are all Your children,
deserving of the love You showed us on the cross. Amen.

The Age of Grace

The Spirit of the Lord GOD is upon me,
because the LORD has anointed me to bring good news . . .
to proclaim the year of the LORD's favor.

ISAIAH 61:1–2 ESV

I opened the kitchen door and gasped in dismay. I hadn't been gone long, yet disaster had occurred in my absence. The refrigerator door stood wide open. Its contents littered the floor. Eggs lay shattered, their yellow yolks trickled from cracked shells. A milk carton lay on its side. The white liquid seeped from its opening making a pool in front of me. Squashed sticks of butter, rashers of bacon, and a half-eaten joint of roast beef lay abandoned in the puddle.

I surveyed the devastation. Then, I realized one thing was missing from the scene. Usually, my English Springer Spaniel puppy would be there to greet me, leaping up and licking my hand. Instead, he sat watching me from his bed in the corner of the room. Only his quivering body and the loud, steady thumping of his tail against the wall told me he was delighted I was home.

"What have you done?" I said sternly. He squirmed. Eventually, he slunk across the floor towards me. I felt his rough tongue on my hand and looked down into big brown eyes that could easily melt the stick of butter lying on the floor beside him. "I'm sorry," they seemed to convey.

I scolded some more as I made a pathway with the mop through the milk. I shook my finger at my puppy as I scooped up broken egg. Yet, I couldn't stay angry for long. I knew the puckered seal on the refrigerator door needed replacing. I understood the smell of succulent beef wafting through the crack in the door had been too powerful a temptation for a sensitive nose. While I did attach a child-proof lock to the refrigerator door the next day, disapproving words were the most I could manage. I couldn't help but offer grace to my pup.

At the beginning of His ministry, Jesus announced that with Him began the age of God's overwhelming kindness. Jesus said He fulfilled the words from the beginning of Isaiah 61. He brought good news for all people, everywhere. Jesus said whoever repented and turned to Him would be forgiven for their sins. Even though they deserved punishment, God had stepped in and sent Jesus to receive the penalty for wrongs committed.

The good news is for us, too. Whatever mess we have made in life, Jesus has taken the retribution we deserve. Whatever we've done, God offers us forgiveness through Jesus Christ. Just like I showed leniency toward my dog, God shows graciousness to us. We are living in the time of God's grace. Make the most of this precious gift—enjoy it for yourself and share God's favor with others.

Heavenly Father, thank You for Your acceptance
and forgiveness because Your Son has taken
the punishment in my place. Amen.

Dogged Determination

Blessed is the one who perseveres under trial because, having stood the test, that person will receive the crown of life that the Lord has promised to those who love him.

JAMES 1:12 NIV

I opened the patio door and felt a brush of fur whiz past my ankles. Our eight-pound Yorkie escape artist was at it again. She hopped like a rabbit down the steps to the backyard, and raced to the rear property line.

"Cupcake! Cupcake!" I yelled her name a few times, but knew I couldn't keep up. I decided to keep watch from above. It was a beautiful spring day. I understood why she wanted to be outside.

But the bright day turned dark in a flash. Duchess, the cantankerous German Shepherd that lived behind us, noticed Cupcake and decided to patrol the border. She darted out her backdoor toward my little Yorkie.

What did my ferocious teacup dog do? She bolted straight at her, barking as if headed for battle. When the two came face to face, Duchess attacked. She bit into poor Cupcake's neck and then threw her a good twenty feet across our lawn.

I did what any fourteen-year-old would do: I screamed hysterically. Duchess's owner called her dog back in and I rushed down to the yard to pick up my injured pup. Cupcake whimpered as blood poured out of her back. I worried she'd never be the same if she somehow lived through this.

Yet, my worry deemed unnecessary. Cupcake was a fighter. Though the veterinarian assessed her injury as fatal, Cupcake endured. She had a determined, unstoppable spirit. Although she clearly could have lost the battle, she didn't give up. She bounced back.

Even years later, Cupcake didn't fear facing Duchess. She growled and barked at her, strategically attacking from the confines of the living room window. She wasn't finished in that fight. If both dogs were out back and Cupcake observed Duchess to be safely leashed, she'd race right back to that property line and yap her disapproval.

That pup taught me the meaning of "dogged determination." An eight-pound David facing her own Goliath, she never stopped barking. Her scars couldn't steal her spirit.

How many times do I face adversity and decide to hide under the covers? Setbacks—from disagreements with friends to disappointments over failed plans—can make me feel like I never want to face the world again. I lick my wounds, hide, and attempt to forget those who've hurt me. I keep my distance from others to prevent them from causing me any future pain. But God calls me to love. He strengthens me to engage again. When relationships feel rocky or my own plans for success fail, He alone is my security and shield.

Lord, help me to keep fighting even after I'm knocked down
and remind me that You are always there
to catch me and heal my wounds so I can persevere
for Your name sake. Amen.

King's Routine

The very hairs of your head are all numbered.
So do not fear; you are more valuable than many sparrows.

MATTHEW 10:30-31 NASB

My cousin and his family had lived beside my grandmother, whom we all called "Mamaw," for a few years, keeping watch over her. They ended up having to move but were unable to take their dog with them. So King, a stunning Alaskan Malamute, became her dog by default. Not long after, my parents and I moved next door to Mamaw. She was getting along in age but insisted on staying in her own house. We were close enough to care for her when she would let us.

The design of Mamaw's small home was unique. Large picture windows stretched across her living room with another large window in the kitchen. All of these windows faced the front yard, which resembled a football field. We soon noticed King had a routine in the yard. He would start the day near the living room windows and then move near the kitchen window. He repeated this pattern, back and forth, all day long. We wondered why he moved around in this way, and one day I figured it out.

That morning I decided to check on Mamaw, and I found her at her usual spot, sitting on the couch in the living room working on her crochet project. Before long she got up to go to the kitchen for something to drink, and I looked out the window. King got up and moved toward the kitchen as well. He remained at that spot in the yard until she returned to the living room and he also returned to his previous post.

The reason for King's routine became evident—he was following Mamaw as she moved through the house!

From that point on, when we were busy at our home but wanted to know where Mamaw was, we would check King's position in the yard. Wherever she was, you would find him, keeping track of her every move. Mamaw even took delight in his care, and it seemed to give her comfort knowing someone was watching over her.

Just as there was nowhere Mamaw could go that King would not follow, there's nowhere on earth I can go to escape God's watchful eye. I can trace His sovereign hand and care all the way through my life, even when I was not following Him. From place to place, He has been with me, and He still is, guiding my life path. I am reminded of one of my favorite hymns, "His Eye is on the Sparrow," and I often tear up when I hear the line "I know He watches me." If His eye notices the tiny sparrow and its every move, how much more does He notice me as I navigate this sometimes crazy life?

Lord, no matter where I go, continue to watch over me
and guide me on the right path. Amen.

Reassuring Presence

We know that God causes everything to work together
for the good of those who love God and are called
according to his purpose for them.

ROMANS 8:28 NLT

It might seem hard to believe that Dan, a Marine veteran, an avid runner and triathlete, suffers from Post-Traumatic Stress Disorder. His broad smile and positive attitude paint a different picture. But pull up a chair and Dan will tell you how he lost part of his leg in combat, and how a very special dog helped him get his life back.

"I remember hearing there's going to be an ambush," Dan said. "I was on top of the .50 cal machine gun. I heard a big explosion. From there it was like slow motion, what you see in the movies. It was a nightmare."

The trauma of that day forever changed Dan, marking him physically and emotionally. When he returned home to his parents and fiancée, Dan just wasn't the same. He began to avoid people, especially crowds, and he struggled with anxiety. He could no longer handle loud noises, as they triggered his PTSD.

"I was always looking over my shoulder wondering if something was going to happen."

One day something major did happen—he was ambushed again. When Dan met his therapy dog, she jumped him, licked his face, and knocked him to the ground. Wally, a black Labrador Retriever, helped Dan engage in society again. The dog's presence helped Dan cope with the discomfort of crowds.

"I didn't want to lay around and say, hey, I'm missing a leg," Dan recalled. "I wanted to make the most of it. Wally was the missing piece physically and mentally."

Wally helped Dan overcome the trauma of war, but the bond these two forged over the years runs deeper. For instance, when Dan suffers from migraines, Wally offers his support in the form of a quiet presence. The pair go everywhere together. The Labrador Retriever even stood watch at the hospital the day Dan's first son was born.

"Wally taught me patience. He taught me loyalty. He taught me how to be myself again."

In Christ, we can experience the same patience and devotion that Dan felt. When we allow God's love to saturate us, we find confidence to be ourselves, complete in God's love. Wally's life and loyalty also illustrates the even deeper loyalty of God, who gave up His Son's life so that we could live.

On Dan's worst days, Wally has a way of looking up at Dan with an expression that seems to say, "Everything is going to be just fine." Wally's never-ending presence in Dan's life reflects how the Holy Spirit calms and reassures us. We can rest knowing that God is always working behind the scenes to redeem every situation.

Lord, help me experience Your presence and trust
in Your ability to work out all things for my good. Amen.

Digging Up Seed

Death and life are in the power of the tongue,
and those who love it will eat its fruits.

PROVERBS 18:21 ESV

I've owned and loved Dachshunds all my life. They are my very favorite breed, but they do have a few characteristics that aren't so endearing, such as their incessant digging. Every Doxie we've ever loved has been a digger, but none quite as proficient as Miller, our black and tan long-haired Dachshund who passed away a few years ago. He lived and loved to dig, and this got him into a lot of trouble with my husband, Jeff.

My husband is quite the landscape artist. He would take hours positioning all of his carefully selected plants in our backyard, only to discover later that Miller had skillfully dug all of them up as only a Dachshund could do. Sometimes I'd be sitting at my writing desk in the sunroom which has a partial view of the backyard, and all I would see was dirt flying, and I knew Miller was at it again. No matter how many times you scolded him, he went right back at it. He was born to dig, and that's what he did.

Apparently, that's what I sometimes do as well. Our pastor was preaching a sermon series on sowing and reaping, and he looked at the congregation one Sunday morning and hollered, "Stop digging up your seed with your words! I can see the dirt flying from here." Jeff elbowed me so hard I almost fell out of my chair, and I understood why. Just the day before, I'd been going on and on about the state of our finances and how no matter how hard we worked, we always seemed to be in the red. Instead of proclaiming my Bible promises concerning our situation such as: my God will provide all of our needs (Philippians 4:19); my Father owns the cattle on a thousand hills (Psalm 50:10); and when I delight in Him, He will give me the desires of my heart (Psalm 37:4). I just bellyached about our current lack of funds. Yes, the dirt was flying.

Ever since that Sunday morning, whenever someone in the family begins digging up their seed with their words, we call it "having a Miller moment." And, every time I'm guilty of going on a digging rampage, I remember our beloved Miller and his digging ways, and I have to smile.

I think bringing Miller's digging escapades to my mind is God's way of gently correcting me in this area. So, let me ask: Are your nails dirty? Have you been digging up your seed with your words? If so, ask the Holy Spirit to show you how the dirt flies. Remember that every word you speak is a seed. And may every seed produce a bountiful crop of faithfulness.

Father, help me to sow seeds of Your promises with my words.
Watch over what I say and help me to stop
digging up my seeds. Amen.

A Grief Shared

Be merciful, just as your Father is merciful.

LUKE 6:36 NIV

Belle, a white Peekapoo with a horrific underbite, had big, sad eyes. Originally dark brown, her eyes had clouded blue with cataracts. Although Belle was not blind, the blue in her eyes gave her an unfocused look, as if she were looking into some distant space no one else could see. And maybe she did.

Belle had lived with one companion for most of her thirteen years—an adoring woman who pampered Belle, giving her everything. In return, Belle had been a devoted and cheery friend whose presence had been a comfort over the years. But her companion's terminal illness meant Belle had to go to a foster home. There she stood in the corner of her crate and barely ate. The only time she left the crate was to go outside to take care of business. She'd sometimes stand in the sun for a few moments, but never long.

The foster home knew Belle grieved deeply, and they did not believe anyone would adopt her. Then they got a call from a woman who had just lost her mother. She was hoping to find a kind, quiet companion, and she chose Belle. The two fit well together, and her new friend quickly found out that Belle did indeed like being outside.

In the next few weeks, long, easy walks in the sun and quiet afternoons on the couch together began to ease the grief of Belle as well as her new companion. Belle became a bit more spry, even at the age of thirteen, enjoying car rides, barking at squirrels, and growling at strangers. But the walks grew ever slower and shorter, the naps longer.

And Belle still did not eat well, refusing more than a morsel at each meal. Her veterinarian thought perhaps her teeth needed work. At her age, some were probably beginning to decay in a way that might not be immediately obvious. The plan was to put her to sleep to do the cleaning and removals. But Belle's aging heart did not tolerate the anesthetic and she passed away on the table.

The vet was devastated. She'd never lost an animal in that way. Belle's companion, however, reassured her. Their short time together had been one of shared mercy. They had found each other when both needed a friend to walk through a hard transition.

Trials come to every life, and we never truly can understand what someone else is going through. But God's love and mercy changes lives, and it brings reassurance and comfort in times of need. If we reach out with our time, our presence, and God's love, healing can come to us all.

*Father, guide me as I turn toward others who are suffering,
and help me show them the same mercy
and kindness You have shown me. Amen.*

Being a Buddy

Barnabas went to Tarsus to look for Saul,
and when he found him, he brought him to Antioch.
So for a whole year Barnabas and Saul met with the church
and taught great numbers of people.

ACTS 11:25-26 NIV

When I was ten, a neighbor asked me to feed JoJo, their painfully shy Brittany Springer Spaniel. Every time I went to feed him, he kept a safe distance. After a few days, he followed me home. Like a stalker, he stayed about twenty to thirty feet away, yet he'd tag along everywhere I went. Eventually, he warmed up and allowed me to pet him.

One day while I played in the front yard, my dad arrived home. As he climbed out of the truck, JoJo bolted like he thought my dad would hurt him. Needless to say, we were shocked at his reaction. Another time, my dad picked up the newspaper and JoJo cowered like he expected a beating. We concluded that at some point a man must have abused him with a newspaper.

JoJo became my bud. He followed me everywhere. Over time, he did warm up to other kids and women, but he mostly cowered or ran from men. About a year later, my family adopted Trouble, a black Lab-Husky mix puppy. At first, JoJo kept his distance, but after Trouble grew a bit, the two became best friends. JoJo played the role of big brother, protecting Trouble in dog scrimmages, and since Trouble loved my dad, JoJo began to trust him too.

Similarly, the Bible often teaches about the importance of friendships. Acts 4:36–37 tells us "Joseph, a Levite from Cyprus, whom the apostles called Barnabas (which means 'son of encouragement'), sold a field he owned and brought the money and put it at the apostles' feet" (NIV). This is the same man who stood before the disciples and vouched for Saul's conversion and his fearless preaching (Acts 9:27). Barnabas and Saul took their ministry on the road to spread the Good News especially to the Gentiles.

I can't help but compare JoJo and Barnabas. They both show the importance of encouraging, helping, and sharing in each other's lives. Friendships also have their ups and downs. JoJo and Trouble, like Barnabas and Saul, didn't always get along perfectly. Yet their friendship through the years is a testimony to the value of deep relationships in life.

As I consider this I have to ask myself, am I being a good friend? Am I a Barnabas in someone's life? Do I need to take more time to nurture any of my current relationships? Is God leading me to befriend someone who could use some encouragement? After all, these special relationships offer a double blessing—the joy of having a buddy and being a buddy to someone else.

Thank you, Father for great examples of friendship I see in everyday life and in Your Word. Open my eyes to all the opportunities of friendship You send my way. Amen.

God Searches for Us

You will feel secure, because there is hope;
you will look around and take your rest in security.

JOB 11:18 ESV

My friend, Dianna, is passionate about rescuing dogs and often fosters a canine for a predetermined period of time. Sometimes the animal shelter is overcrowded and other times a dog shows signs of stress in the close environment. Many people select the most appealing pup when choosing a pet, but Dianna searches for what seems to be the most unlovable mutt who needs her attention the most.

One day, a shelter worker gave Dianna and her husband a tour of the crowded facility so she could decide which dog to take home for a few weeks. As Dianna scrutinized each face to determine which pooch might need a break from the shelter, she noticed a cage in the corner that had been ignored. In the shadows, she'd almost missed the black trembling ball.

"What about this dog?" Dianna said.

"That's Miss Ellie," the worker said. "I forgot about her."

"Is she available to foster?" Dianna asked.

"That'd be great! But I'll warn you, Miss Ellie is afraid of her own shadow."

"I'll take her," said Dianna, her fingers itching to soothe the frightened girl.

Miss Ellie seemed to embrace Dianna as she nuzzled her doggie nose into my friend's neck. After half an hour of petting, the dog's trembling stopped and they left the shelter behind. When they arrived home, Dianna opened the truck door and Miss Ellis leaped from the cab and investigated every inch of the large, fenced-in yard. Then she returned to Dianna, and looked up with soulful eyes that seemed to say, "Thank you for saving me." Then Miss Ellie snuggled up on Dianna's lap, sighed, and went to sleep. In that instant, Dianna knew. Miss Ellie would be a foster failure: she would never be returned to the shelter. She had found a home.

There are many, like Miss Ellie, who live in darkness, hiding in the shadows, afraid to trust anyone. But the Savior comes and seeks us in the darkest corners, even when others seem to have forgotten about us.

God will wait patiently, until you are ready to trust Him. Once you accept His love and forgiveness there is no need to fear. You will never be alone again and He will meet your every need.

Step into the light and leave darkness and fear behind. When we call Him Master, our lives transform, and regardless of our circumstances, we can discover joy, hope, and a forever home in our Savior's loving arms. Jesus loves you so much He suffered and died on the cross for you and for me, and He overcame the darkness. Trust Jesus and fear no more.

Father, thank You for seeking me out and saving me from the darkness. Please help me shine Your light so that others discover Your loving arms where there is nothing to fear. Amen.

I Choose You

You did not choose me, but I chose you and appointed you
so that you might go and bear fruit—fruit that will last—
and so that whatever you ask in my name
the Father will give you.

JOHN 15:16 NIV

Some dogs are just extra special. Blue was that way. It wasn't that he was a high-pedigree purebred. It wasn't that he was particularly beautiful. It wasn't even that we picked him out from all the other dogs in the pound.

Blue picked us.

Even though we live in the country, three dogs seemed like enough. So when Blue flattened his cute little puppy body against the gravel in our driveway to scoot under the metal gate to our property, we stood firm. Even our other dogs didn't want him inside the fence. My husband gently opened the gate and put Blue outside, then blocked his entry spot by putting logs in front of the gate. *That should take care of that*, we thought to ourselves.

Next thing we knew Blue found another spot. With just a little digging, it became the next point of entry to our yard. Again my hubby put Blue on the other side of the fence and blocked his entry point. I didn't want or need another dog. My dogs didn't want another dog. I had enough people and dogs to take care of. But Blue refused to be rejected.

Time after time Blue was put out of the yard. And every time, he found a new way to get in. Eventually, we decided

Blue must be meant for us and we let him stay. By that time the older dogs had become tolerant of his presence.

Not long after Blue became part of the family, we learned that Moose, our mixed breed, happy-go-lucky, beautiful-blonde-bundle-of-love dog, had cancer. Moose had been part of the family a long time. His diagnosis was devastating.

When Moose died, an interesting thing happened. Blue took on some of Moose's personality traits and endearing habits. It wasn't long before Blue had totally stepped up into Moose's place in the family. And to think, I almost rejected him.

Don't we treat God the same way? He tries to provide us with exactly what we need and we reject it. We throw it out, close the spot where it came into our lives, and try to move on as if it never presented itself.

When we are finally exhausted and realize we are never going to be able to solve our own problem, we take a step back and invite God, usually beg Him, to come into our lives and be part of the solution. We discover God's initial provision was the perfect answer to our problem all along.

Blue's journey into our lives continuously reminds us of God's provision and His never-giving-up love that should never be rejected.

Lord, give us wisdom to accept without question
the gifts You provide for us. Amen.

The Prodigal Puppy

Where can I go from Your Spirit?
Or where can I flee from Your presence?

PSALM 139:7 NKJV

Buckshot, our Beagle-Labrador Retriever, was just a puppy when he dug under the fence in our backyard for the first—and only—time. Even though I looked all through the yard for him, it wasn't until I called his name that I heard him whimper. The sound led me to the freshly dug hole under the fence, and I knew where he'd escaped to.

When I found Buckshot, his back was pressed against the outside of our fence, his head was tilted upward, and his pitiful howl pierced the air. Caught in the brambles, he was trapped and unable to come to me. He watched as I made my way through the thorns to reach him. Once I held my prodigal puppy in my arms, he ceased his cries, relaxed his body, and snuggled close.

My puppy wanted his freedom. He wanted to leave the confines of our yard and explore what was on the other side of our fence. Unaware of the brambles and thorns that waited for him, Buckshot wanted to experience the outside world on his own. Once he managed to escape, he found himself in a sticky situation he couldn't remedy on his own. How could he undo what he'd done? Much like the prodigal son in the parable Jesus told, things didn't work out the way Buckshot planned.

The parable of the prodigal son in the Gospels speaks of a person with a similar mindset as Buckshot. This son wanted to escape the confines of life with his father and brother. He wanted to explore the world on the other side of the land. Although the prospects of a different life seemed appealing at first, the son was not prepared for the brambles and thorns that entangled him. In his distress, the prodigal realized his mistake and returned home to where he cried out to his father who came running to meet him.

Perhaps, like Buckshot and the prodigal son, we want our freedom from the confines of the perimeters God set for us. His Word describes how to live a joyful and fulfilling life within a set of standards, and perhaps we feel constricted and long to explore what is on the other side of the fence. We may even run away from God, but in our leaving we run into brambles and thorns that snarl and entangle us. In our distress we cry out. And our heavenly Father, who never stopped searching for us, hears our cries and comes to where we are. He wraps us in His loving arms and tells us how much we were missed and how glad He is that we are found.

Father, when I strain against Your loving confines and want to run from You, help me realize there is nowhere I can go that You are not already there, patiently waiting for me to come back to You. Amen.

Counter Cruising Crimes

*I don't really understand myself, for I want to do what is right,
but I don't do it. Instead, I do what I hate.*

ROMANS 7:15 NLT

My refrigerator and Airedale Terrier pup arrived around the same time. The appliance came with an estimated cost of annual operation. The dog did not.

After only two days, Amelia wracked up several hundred dollars in vet bills due to an intestinal parasite. The medication and special food restored her to health and she grew strong enough to knock my bedroom closet door off the track.

I never kept a record of the shoes and socks destroyed but had to accept blame myself for not being more careful about leaving tempting items within her reach. I thought I had outsmarted her by the time she grew tall enough to reach the countertops.

My sister-in-law spent a few days with me and agreed to prepare supper on a day I had to work. I anticipated a wonderful meal from this gourmet cook who never had a dog. When I arrived home and peered under the foil covering the roasting pan on the stove, I was surprised to find it empty. The delicious meal I anticipated had evaporated with tomorrow's sandwich I'd hoped to carry for lunch.

Interrupting the cook reading a book, I inquired about the turkey breast. I took notice of the glasses she wore, knowing she was like me, a contact lenses wearer. Not only had the dog eaten the whole turkey breast, she'd also eaten the lens case retrieved off the bathroom counter with the lenses still inside.

Added to lifetime operating costs, we had to repair a dining room chair, pharmaceutically treat ehrlichiosis, and purchase hundreds of gallons of cleaning products required to sanitize the floor after she developed pancreatitis. In spite of her mishaps, she was a great companion during healthy periods. She'd hung her head many times after an infraction and inched her way back into my heart afterward. The look in her eyes revealed remorse but her behavior got the best of her almost every time.

On the day she passed away, I had prepared a large dinner for my out-of-town family. They arrived and old Amelia rose and went to their car for a greeting. As the last relative entered the house, I noticed Amelia stagger and lay down. After fifteen minutes, as I knelt at her side forgiving her of everything, she passed on. It was like she waited to say goodbye to family.

I'm so grateful my heavenly Father is more loving and forgiving than I can ever be. I've tested His patience and have interrupted His plans more than once. Yet, He lifts my head and forgives. And the cost is all on Him.

Lord, I can do nothing good without You,
and I come for mercy and help in my times of need. Amen.

Stand Your Ground

Be strong and courageous.
Do not be frightened, and do not be dismayed,
for the LORD your God is with you wherever you go.

JOSHUA 1:9 ESV

As most people know, we can learn a lot from watching our dogs. Even courage in the face of danger, as I did one summer from a dog who seldom barked.

Lassie was, of course, a Collie. She belonged to our neighbors and was as beautiful a dog as I've ever known. She had the typical Collie temperament—sweet, gentle, and usually quiet. In fact, I had known her more than a year before I heard the sound of her voice. I didn't mind, however, because I had been sternly warned. If Lassie barked, we were to run to the closest place of safety because Lassie only barked at venomous snakes. No one knew why.

Likewise, no one knew how she could tell the venomous ones from the non-venomous. But she could, and when her barks echoed throughout the pine woods where we lived, kids would scatter in all directions away from her as the adults ran toward her, most of them carrying a hoe. Lassie would bark for several minutes, then—if no one appeared to handle the danger—she'd attack the snake herself.

No one wanted her to get bitten; luckily she never did. This normally placid and loyal dog had more courage than I'd ever seen, and she knew how to handle snakes. She would actually appear to be disappointed if a human took care of a snake before she had a chance to. And while she only barked at snakes, over time I saw her stand down strangers, aggressive dogs, and, one particular time, a cow.

Lassie would quietly but firmly shove her way between the danger and her human companions. Courageous but never foolish, anytime Lassie took a stand, she did so warily and wisely. From her, I learned to stand my ground but not to rush into anything.

Over time, I learned that evaluating a situation and standing our ground in the face of opposition is exactly what God expects of us as well. He is always with us; He goes where we do. Even more so, when we follow His chosen path for us, He'll equip us for the journey no matter what it takes, and He will show us a way around or through all difficulties.

Lord, because of Your presence, I can stand courageous
in the face of any obstacle. Guide me and help me remember
that with You, I can stand my ground. Amen.

Pixie's Prize

*Oil and perfume make the heart glad, and the sweetness
of a friend comes from his earnest counsel.*

PROVERBS 27:9 ESV

Pixie was a mixed-breed puppy my brother found in a box beside the road when we were young. "Pretty" did not describe this dog with long, multi-colored hair and front teeth protruding from her lower jaw. She had one blue eye and one brown eye, which added to her odd appearance.

I often wondered if she had been abandoned because of her looks. It broke my heart that someone had left her like that, but Pixie found her forever home with us. Because we loved our sweet Pixie, we saw her as beautiful, not ugly.

My neighbor and classmate, Jeanie, had a beautiful Cocker Spaniel with a silky, gold coat and chocolate-brown eyes. When we were together, Jeanie often said how beautiful her dog, Goldie, was and how unattractive Pixie was. To avoid her hurtful comments, I started walking Pixie when I knew Jeanie wouldn't be outside.

One day, though, our paths crossed as we walked our dogs. Jeanie told me she was entering Goldie in a contest sponsored by our local newspaper. I asked my father to find out about the contest so I could enter Pixie. When Daddy listed the categories offered, I settled on one I thought suited Pixie. While Jeanie had entered Goldie in the most beautiful dog category, I entered Pixie in the most unusual dog category.

I often watched Jeanie brush Goldie, making her coat shine like silk. After the brushing, she fastened a pretty bow in the dog's golden locks. No matter how much I brushed Pixie's hair, it never shone like Goldie's. And if I put a bow in her hair, she immediately pulled it out.

The day of the contest I learned there was only one other entrant in the most unusual dog category. When the trophies were handed out, Pixie was proclaimed the winner. Many dogs had been entered in the most beautiful category. When Goldie did not win a prize, Jeanie burst into tears.

A few weeks later, I took Pixie's trophy to show-and-tell at school. When I held it up for the whole class to see, tears rolled down Jeanie's cheeks. After school that day, I asked Jeanie to walk home with me. I kept Pixie's trophy in my book bag because I did not want my classmate to cry again. As we talked, Jeanie asked forgiveness for her unkind words about Pixie. I accepted her apology and a deep friendship developed between us.

What began as a competition became a bridge to a friendship we both treasured. A hurtful experience does not have to drive people apart. Like the aroma of oil and perfume, the fragrance that rises from working out differences pleases God and makes our hearts glad.

Father, thank You for the grace to work out differences and make sweet friendships. Amen.

A Comforting Companion

God is our merciful Father and the source of all comfort.
He comforts us in all our troubles so that we can comfort others.

2 CORINTHIANS 1:3-4 NLT

People usually rescue dogs, but sometimes dogs rescue people.

It was a Thursday morning when the police broke the news to Deena—news no mother ever wants to hear. Her twenty-one-year-old son, Tyler, had died in a car crash a few hours earlier. His life, which overflowed with possibilities, came to a sudden halt that day, leaving his mom devastated.

In the coming months depression took over, holding Deena's life in a death grip. After the funeral and the initial support subsided, grief drove Deena into her room. The veil of sleep and a closed door became her solace and way to cope.

A special mixed-breed bird dog, however, crept her way past Deena's defenses. Sadie, the product of a rescue herself, became the rescuer, finding a way to pierce through the dark, searing pain. By nosing Deena's door open and hopping onto her bed, the dog would curl up next to Deena for hours, emanating comfort. The puppy had found a way to help ease the pain.

"It's like Sadie helped to absorb her grief," said Deena's friend.

When Deena sat on the couch, Sadie—without fail—nestled at her feet. The puppy trailed her on jaunts to the kitchen. She offered near-constant companionship through the unbearable sorrow. Though the dog belonged to Deena's roommate, Sadie migrated into Deena's room at night. She traded her regular spot next to her owner's bed to be at Deena's side. Sadie seemed to show a human-like compassion and a beyond-human ability to sense grief.

The bird dog also managed to coax Deena outside to play fetch. Deena found humor in the puppy's antics, especially the way Sadie would train her eyes on the ball and not let up for hours. Slowly, Deena's laughter—an almost foreign sound—began to fill the house again.

This unwavering loyalty helped Deena catch a glimpse of the God of all comfort. God sees us in our seasons of pain and loss. He speaks to us through His Word, the kindness of people, and yes, sometimes through the love of dogs. Even in prolonged mourning and grief, God promises never to leave us, never to forsake us. God longs to mend every single broken place in our lives. Like a good parent, God will use whatever means it takes to communicate His love to His children.

This is the love Jesus extended with His arms open wide on the cross. It chases us down and shines light even into our darkness. Take a few minutes to dwell in this love. Open your heart to the God who is love and receive the peace, comfort, and joy only He can bring.

Jesus, open my eyes to Your comforting peace and give me the ability to see just how much You really love me. Amen.

Lessons in Friendship

A friend loves at all times.

PROVERBS 17:17 NIV

She wasn't much to look at, but to me Penny was a beautiful Dachshund. She was supposed to be of the miniature version, but I think I shared one too many cookies with her. Penny and I grew up together. While she was wetting the carpets in the house, I was wetting my diapers. We quickly became best buddies. She was a great playmate. Sometimes, I'd tie a bonnet on Penny's head and drape pearls around her neck. Then I'd put on my floppy hat and my mother's high heels, and we'd have tea parties. Of course, I'd pour real water in Penny's cup and give myself imaginary tea. It was always great fun, as Penny was the perfect guest.

Other times, Penny and I would sit in my sandbox and make up stories. I would tell her all about the princes and princesses who lived in my tree house. And sometimes, I would make up stories about her. She liked it when I would mention her name every so often. She would wag her tail and give me a lick as if to say, "That's good. Go on."

Penny was a great cheerleader too. When my dad taught me to ride my bike in the alley behind our house, Penny would bark and run in circles, cheering me on to a no-training-wheels life. When I would fall and scrape my knee, which I often did, Penny would run to my side and lick away the tears. She was always right by my side.

As years went by and I grew, our friendship grew too. Penny was no longer my playmate in the sandbox; she had become my sounding board. I went on and on about math class, cheer-leading practice, and that cute boy who sat next to me in study hall, and Penny would cock her head with great interest. She was also my greatest ally. When my parents grounded me from the eighth grade dance, the most important social event of the year, Penny stayed with me inside my room. She cuddled up next to me and let me cry myself to sleep.

She was the perfect best friend. She didn't have a huge vocabulary, but her eyes and tail wags spoke volumes. If dogs go to heaven, she definitely made it.

Dogs teach us so much about friendship, don't they? They are loyal, kind, attentive, loving, selfless, protective, and fun. We can learn so much from our canine companions. I once read that "dog" is "God" spelled backwards, and that wasn't by coincidence. The writer went on to say it was because dogs have so many godly attributes. I would have to agree.

May we all be as faithful in friendship as the dogs we love. Let's face it: they have set the bar pretty high.

Father, help us to be as loyal, kind, loving,
and selfless as the dogs You've allowed us to love. Amen.

He Shows Us
the Father

*In the past God spoke to our ancestors through the prophets
at many times and in various ways, but in these last days he has
spoken to us by his Son, whom he appointed heir of all things,
and through whom also he made the universe.*

HEBREWS 1:1–2 NIV

I caught a glimpse of a golden Chow Chow as I drove by the roadside park. I didn't think much about it. We lived in a rural area, and strays and abandoned dogs were common. But a couple days later the dog was still there. On my way back to town, I pulled into the picnic area. The dog was sitting under a tree. He looked thin, and his coat was matted with burs. I eased cautiously out of my car, watching to see what he would do. As soon as I stepped around the door, the dog sprang up and shot off into the nearby pasture.

I went back the next day with some treats and a pan of water. Again, the dog fled as soon as he saw me emerge from the car. I made several visits to the park over the next few weeks, but the dog never let me approach. I tried sitting on the ground to let him get used to my presence, but he resolutely stayed on the opposite side of the park. As I sat there one day I found myself wishing I could speak dog. If I could speak his language, maybe I could make him understand he had a chance for a better life than the park. How could I convey it? Food. Water. Safety. Home.

God wanted to speak to us in a way we could understand so

He sent Jesus. In the incarnation, Jesus wrapped His divinity in human form and came to show us what God is like. He walked down dusty roads. He went to weddings. He broke bread with His disciples. He got tired and hungry. But He also showed us the Father. He showed us God's compassion and mercy. He showed us God's justice and power. He revealed God's heart for the downtrodden, and His heartbreak over the people's rejection of Him. He demonstrated God's sacrificial love and proved His power over death and the grave. God spoke to us in our language through Jesus, and Jesus showed us the Father.

Even when we flee from Him, Jesus makes His home in our midst to show us the depth and power of God's mercy and grace. Jesus came to show us that there is a better way than the lostness of our sin. He points the way to our loving Father, who waits to bind up our wounds and welcome us home. If we want to know what God is like, we only need to look to Jesus.

Lord, thank You that You weren't content
to leave me lost and wandering in my sin;
You showed me the way home through Your Son. Amen.

Friendship

Two are better than one, because they have a good return
for their labor: If either of them falls down,
one can help the other up. But pity anyone
who falls and has no one to help them up.

ECCLESIASTES 4:9-10 NIV

When my son, an avid duck hunter, announced he'd bought two dogs, I expected the breed to be a Retriever or water dog. To my surprise, his new puppies were Dachshunds named Penelope and Fiona. It was then I realized the seriousness of his relationship with the woman who is now his wife. "Wiener dogs" had been a part of her childhood home.

Penelope's slick coat is the color of coal, but her brows and snout are caramel colored. Fiona has long, flowing hair that matches pumpkin bread with raisins. Every time I see those two dogs with broad chests and long, sausage-shaped bodies running on stubby legs, I smile. Not your typical bird dog, but they are known for going after badger and rabbits.

What I admire most about these two girls is their adoration for each other and their people, my son and daughter-in-law. These girls spend their days sleeping and playing together and lavishing love on their family. It's a joy to see them romp and play, side by side, investigating their small world, and playing tug-o-war with a rope.

Recently, Fiona suffered complications from a complex surgery, and one might have thought Penelope also ill by her mournful face. Her dark eyes showed such compassion and concern for her best friend when they touched noses.

Thankfully, Fiona recovered and the two are up to their usual tricks. What a blessing it is to have a best friend. Someone who understands and cares for us.

Everyone needs a helpmate because any difficult task is made easier when shared. Holding a friend's hand when we're walking through life's valleys makes the journey less difficult. Adam was given Eve as a helpmate, Moses had his brother Aaron to lean on, God sent Samuel to Eli when his sons failed him, and Naomi lost her sons but God provided Ruth as a daughter. Paul planted and Apollos watered. Jesus sent the disciples out to work in pairs when more than twice the ground could have been covered if He'd sent them out individually. He knew each one needed a friend to lift him up if he stumbled.

Joy is multiplied and labor is divided when we have a friend on the journey. Also consider this: "For where two or three gather in my name, there am I with them" (Matthew 18:20 NIV). Jesus will send you the helpmate you need if you ask Him. He knows exactly what you need.

Father, thank You for sending me helpmates to carry out
Your work, and no matter where I go or what I do,
I know You are always with me. Amen.

Stay Out of the Mud

He does not punish us for all our sins;
he does not deal harshly with us, as we deserve.

PSALM 103:10 NLT

Kirby was an absolute mess. Our German Shepherd-Golden Retriever, found a mud hole in the back yard—courtesy of the soaker hose with a pinhole leak—and decided to roll around in the mud. She was covered from muzzle to tail. And she wanted in.

I reluctantly let Kirby inside the laundry room. She was filthy. Still, she was my dog and I loved her. Kirby looked repentant. She looked sorrowful. She looked at me as if she hoped I'd be merciful instead of treating her as she deserved. I'm sure it was a momentary lapse of good judgment on her part. Besides, I imagine Kirby's frolic in the oozy mud brought her pleasure on a hot summer's day—until she saw me, that is.

As much as the sight of Kirby covered in mud irritated me, and I knew it would cost me something to remove the filth from her, I couldn't stay upset with my dog. Because, you see, I've wallowed around in mud holes of my own. Can you relate?

It certainly isn't something I go around looking to do. I don't intend to cover myself with yuck. I get caught up in the moment. It's a momentary lapse of reasoning. I forget who I am. I forget whose I am. I forget I belong to a Holy God and called to a life of righteousness. My mud romp seems enjoyable for the moment until I face my Master and realize how far I've strayed from the standard He set before me.

That's when I realize I've missed the mark and sinned. I am sorrowful. I am repentant. There is nothing I can do on my own to clean myself up from my mess. So I fall on the mercy and grace of a God who does not punish me as I deserve, a God who casts my sins away as far as the east is from the west.

Fortunately, God does not wait for me to get all the mud off before He lets me enter His presence. God washes me clean through the power of the sacrificial blood of His Son, Jesus. Jesus—my risen Savior, Lord, Messiah, Redeemer, and King. He is the Lamb who was slain. It is only by Christ's wounds I am healed, washed whiter than snow, cleansed, and found not guilty.

The next time I find myself tempted by the temporary enjoyment of a mud hole, I will plan to not linger near it. Instead, I'll pray for the strength to avoid it and run as far away as possible.

Father, thank You that You do not treat me as my sins deserve, and because of Christ's sacrifice on the cross, all the muddy stains of my wrongdoings are washed away. Amen.

Jezebel
and the Church Ladies

*Let us consider how we may spur one another on
toward love and good deeds.*

HEBREWS 10:24 NIV

For all her life, Nettie had a contrary streak in her a mile wide. Her brothers—and especially her husband—knew that arguing with her was a futile and frustrating experience. She could dig her heels in about something and never move. And once upon a time, this streak kicked in over the name of her dog.

She was a beauty, this little dog, with shiny fur that feathered around her tummy and legs. Black on top with a tan belly, legs, and feet, her calm temperament disguised a joy for life that sent her bounding over the local cornfields and flatwoods. The neighborhood children clustered around her for games and romping about. Everyone loved her.

But in an odd fit of spite, Nettie named this sweetheart Jezebel. This did not sit well with some of the ladies in Nettie's community. Before long, a group of them stood on her porch, wanting answers. Why in the world would she name an animal after the most horrid woman in the Bible?

"To make people talk," Nettie replied. "And you did." They continued to gossip about the little dog, avoiding Nettie in town and giving her sideways glances at church. Obviously, if Nettie named a beloved dog for that woman, there was something about Jezebel she admired, something she might even want to emulate.

Finally, Nettie's sister-in-law took her aside. Her brother's sweet wife was a devout woman of God who had studied the Bible all her life. "You've proved a point," she told Nettie, "but you missed a bigger one. As believers, we're supposed to inspire our neighbors to be their best, not their worst. They'll show their worst nature in their own time, but we shouldn't drive them to it." She suggested Nettie read Paul's words in Romans 14:13 and 1 Corinthians 8:13. "You're making them stumble, which is just as bad as what they're doing."

Nettie had to think about that for a bit. Sometimes a stubborn streak isn't easy to set aside. But eventually, Paul's words settled on her heart. And the little black and tan dog spent the rest of her life as Lulubelle.

Seeing the flaws in others is much easier than seeing them in ourselves. That's human nature. But throughout God's Word there are reminders to examine our own hearts before we make judgments on those around us. God knows the heart of every person, and He will eventually judge them by what He sees there. Until then, we are called to inspire them to be the best they can be, not the worst.

Father, forgive me when I cause one of Your children to stumble.
Help me to see the best in them and bring that out
by showing them Your love and mercy. Amen.

Steadfast Friends

"Abraham believed God, and it was counted to him
as righteousness"—and he was called a friend of God.

JAMES 2:23 ESV

B'ie, sit!" Two-year-old Addi pointed her finger. "B'ie, sit!" she repeated.

Addi sat on top of the dinner table. She had spotted the treat box and climbed up to get her favorite pet a treat. A brindle Boxer, Brie loved the sweet little girl. Whether or not Addi could say her words properly, "B'ie" always seemed to understand.

Walking over to the table, Brie looked up at Addi and sat. Addi scooted to the edge and tossed the dog biscuit to Brie. Brie crunched for a moment, swallowed, and promptly sat again. Addi reached into the box and threw Brie another treat.

As Brie crunched her treat, Mom came into the room. "Addi, what are you doing on that table?" One look at the box of treats and Addi's mother had a pretty good idea. "Addi, Brie loves for you to play with her. But you need to play with her on the floor. Come down from the table so you won't fall."

Addi slid off the table and toddled after Brie. "B'ie c'mere!" Brie loved to be wherever Addi was and rarely failed to respond to the toddler's call. When she heard her name, she came running to Addi's side. When Addi was learning to walk, she had hooked her little arm around Brie's back, and Addi toddled keep up with her. Brie walked slowly so Addi wouldn't fall. In just a few turns around the room with Brie, Addi had a much steadier gait.

The duo could often be found in the playroom. Brie laid down in the middle of the floor. Addi stretched out on the rug using Brie's stomach for a pillow. The good-natured Boxer seemed to revel in the attention. She was always ready to play with Addi or just sit with her in front of the television. On days when Addi was close to naptime, she called "B'ie" and toddled over to Brie's bed. Both curled up on the overstuffed pillow to sleep.

The friendship Addi and Brie have has grown over the years because they spent time together. They not only played but also just "hung out." Even more special is the bond we can have with our Heavenly Father. God longs for us to be in fellowship with Him—He wants to be friends with us. Our relationship with God is strengthened when we spend time with Him. Studying His Word, talking to Him, or just sitting in His presence takes you to a deeper level with Him every time. That is when you can say with Abraham, "I am a friend of God."

Lord, thank You for the special friendships in my life
and for how You are my most steadfast friend. Amen.

Duke Comes Running

*My sheep hear My voice, and I know them,
and they follow Me.*

JOHN 10:27 NKJV

Duke! Come on, boy!" When I arrive at my parents' house for a visit, I immediately call for Duke when I get out of the car. Duke is a beautiful black Labrador mix who lives up the street from my parents in a small hollow in eastern Kentucky. He is the "neighborhood dog," visiting various houses every day for handouts. Duke is one of the friendliest dogs I have ever encountered as he has never met a stranger, and he seems genuinely excited to see me every time we meet.

All I have to do is yell his name, and he comes running when he hears my voice—a voice Duke knows even though I'm not there very often. Wagging his tail vigorously, he bounds down the yard and greets me. He stops right at my feet and sits down, looking up at me with what seems to be a smile on his face. I "love on him," as we say here in the mountains, and then check to see what my parents might have on hand for him to eat. They usually have a bowl of something waiting for him, and when I put the food out for him he attacks it with the same enthusiasm as he does in greeting us. Once he has his fill, he heads back up the road on another adventure, and I imagine he follows this same routine at each house. You can tell by looking at him that he gets plenty of treats and "loving" everywhere he goes.

Duke knows he will get some attention and something special when he hears my voice. In the same way, I know I will be blessed when I hear the still, small voice of Jesus. Although I yell Duke's name, Jesus's approach is different, speaking tenderly to my spirit in the most loving way possible. Sometimes that voice gives instruction, while other times it comforts me and even corrects me. There are moments when Jesus calls me to action, but some days He calls me to pull back—to step away from the hectic pace of life just to spend time with Him and to listen.

Relationships are a two-way street, a give-and-take. I give Duke treats and he responds with gratefulness. It's the same with Jesus. My prayers often consist of requests for things I need or want, but if I don't take the time to listen and be thankful during prayer, my relationship with Him becomes one-sided and suffers. Jesus wants to know me and wants me to know Him on an intimate level. So I think I will run to Him, sit down at His feet, and spend time in His presence.

Lord, what a wonderful gift it is to know You!
Give me ears to hear Your voice today
and to follow where You lead. Amen.

Yodel Duo

Then you will call upon Me and go and pray to Me,
and I will listen to you.

JEREMIAH 29:12 NKJV

Some have and some haven't, a few absolutely refused and a few have had to be coached, but only one of my Airedale Terriers sang like a pro.

I'd kneel and begin with a high C, which elicited a low, throaty growl. She took the first cue to transition up several octaves till she matched my howl, note for note. Although she never mastered any lyrics, she could howl along in near-perfect harmony with any melody.

As I leaned in closer, the accuracy of her response increased. Miss Pickle nestled into me as she picked up cue number two, lengthening each woof. She might sit or lay, but in either position her neck extended as she howled upward toward an imaginary moon. I really believe she smiled as well.

After a while she could be cued to sing with my husband, even though the score never ranged out of tenor scales. A timid guest might misinterpret growling as a threat, but Miss Pickle never bit anyone. She'd win them with a song and be petted as a reward. And, audible through open windows, our singing inspired my neighbor to accuse me of harboring drunken coyotes.

The songs brought great joy and laughter to our home, and the time invested allowed dog and master to share in an intimate, special activity. When she passed away from kidney failure just before her eighth birthday, her absence left a unique void—a quiet that never could be filled again.

The doggie/master duo is similar to my prayer time with the Lord—a special, intimate relationship shared between follower and Master. I struggle to match His notes as I continually offer praise and petitions to the One who seeks for me to sing along, listening first.

The ballad He sings is written throughout the beautiful lyrics of His Word. Every chapter of harmony, occasional discordant melodies, crescendos of victory, dirges of defeat, and love songs meant to woo or capture, are music to my soul. Like an orchestra warming up, my first cue to begin prayer is to tune up in the Word. I smile and lean into Him, to sense His presence. I might remain on my knees at His feet. I will bow or hold my head high toward a celestial sky and seek to match His notes, knowing He will hear me when I call. The response may come in robust heavenly harmony or silence, my cue to rest and sit out a few stanzas as He conducts the ensemble of my life.

The soprano who sang with Miss Pickle is now a contralto, but I'm grateful for her inspiration to join my voice to the Master, knowing He will listen. My voice has changed but the Master's has not.

Lord, I may sound like a howling dog but I'm thankful
You listen to the voice of my heart. Amen.

Follow In Love

*Those who accept my commandments and obey them
are the ones who love me. And because they love me,
my Father will love them. And I will love them
and reveal myself to each of them.*

JOHN 14:21 NLT

Seeing a working sheepdog is a bit like watching the Olympics. These dogs push the bounds of training, demonstrate extraordinary discipline, and completely mesmerize those who watch.

Along the rolling green hills of Ireland, where sheep roam the countryside, you might glimpse Border Collies like Max hard at work. Max spends his days at Kells Sheep Centre near Dublin, where he loves to show off for the tourists who come to see sheepdogs in action.

There's something beautiful about catching Max and his canine teammates in their element, working for the love of their master. For instance, Max can turn in a flash when he hears his shepherd, Brendan, signal him with a whistle. He rarely misses a command as he zigzags across the fields.

With one whistle, Max drives the sheep left. Another signal sends Max speeding in the other direction, reversing the flock. While another command leaves Max crouching still, allowing the flock some rest.

Not all sheepdogs, however, are trainable. Some lack the willingness to learn, but the ones who submit to training display a stunning ability to perform.

Dogs like Max can move hundreds of sheep across huge distances. In one aerial video of a sheep drive, the flock seems to flow like water through a funnel as the dogs steer the sheep through a tiny gate. If you look closely you'll see the dogs running out an invisible boundary—a line that the flock dares not cross.

Max didn't learn these skills overnight. His training took time—seven months, spread out over the course of a year and a half. "They don't learn it all at once. They learn in stages as they grow ready to learn," Brendan explains.

In much the same way, spiritual training takes time. God never expects us to learn everything all at once, but He teaches us in stages, throughout every season of life. God gently sanctifies us as we grow ready to learn. And our Good Shepherd is infinitely patient with us. In response, following His commands equates to loving Him.

I've realized that just as shepherds cannot train unwilling dogs, God also needs me to submit to His training. What if I could hear and respond to my heavenly Master like Max obeys his shepherd? What could God accomplish if I could spring into action at His first signal? How many wounds could be healed? How many feet could be washed? What would my life look like if I learned to attune my ears to His every call? If I can take this first step, God can accomplish amazing things through me.

Lord Jesus, I submit to You and ask that You train my heart to hear and obey Your commands. Amen.

Spot and
the New Mom

*Aspire to live quietly, and to mind your own affairs, and to work
with your hands, as we instructed you, so that you may walk
properly before outsiders and be dependent on no one.*

1 THESSALONIANS 4:11-12 ESV

Spot, an English setter, had once been a valiant hunting dog. But he now wandered our neighborhood, looking for food and trouble. He usually found both in abundance. We lived in the country, among a scattering of houses over several acres of pine woods, and every afternoon, Spot made the rounds, chasing squirrels and eating other dogs' chow.

This was in a bygone age, and our county had neither leash laws nor an animal control department, so the neighbors tolerated Spot. Kids yelled at and chased him, but Spot would just trot away—until the day he poked his nose where it definitely didn't belong

We just called her Kitty, and she lived in our carport in a box which my mother had lined with an old quilt. Kitty preferred the outdoors, and she was an excellent mouser. Kitty was a no-nonsense, practical cat, half-Siamese and half-traveling cat. She had thick, soft black fur that shone in the sun.

One afternoon, Mother picked me up from school, telling me that Kitty had delivered a litter that morning, so we needed to give her a bit of distance for a few days. But, as we got out of the car at home, we realized that Spot had not given her the same consideration.

He had been eating our dogs' food, just a few steps from the box, when he obviously got a whiff of the new arrivals. He stepped to the box and dropped his head in. He immediately skittered backwards, yelping, a black cat firmly attached to his head. Spot shook his head furiously to no avail. Turning, he rubbed his head on the ground. Kitty let go, only to reattach herself to his rear. Spot raced in circles, at one point even trying to climb a tree. Finally, he galloped full speed toward a grove of trees in his own yard.

A few moments later, Kitty trotted back toward us, a rather satisfied expression on her face. Mother shrugged. "Even the Bible tells us to mind our own business." The whole incident had lasted less than a minute, and Spot never returned to our yard.

Scripture often tells us not to be busybodies or gossips, and in this passage, Paul encourages believers to inspire "outsiders" by how we live. Sometimes we forget that we are the only "Bible" some people see. We best reveal the depth of our faith not by words—and definitely not by "meddling"—but by our behavior, by living and working graciously in the sight of others.

Lord, direct my hands and feet to work well for You.
Help me show others my faith
and Your love by my actions. Amen.

Fruit of the Spirit

*The fruit of the Spirit is love, joy, peace, patience,
kindness, goodness, faithfulness, gentleness, self-control;
against such things there is no law.*

GALATIANS 5:22–23 ESV

A visit from Mr. Johnson never surprised anyone because his beat-up, rusted truck made such a ruckus. Mama often invited him to join us for lunch after church and I'd cringe knowing the meal would be anything but peaceful. His habit of banging his fist to make a point made the whole table shake.

One day, he surprised my family when he visited our farm with a puppy and he spoke just above a whisper, "This is Rex." Linda, a waitress at the truck stop where he regularly ate breakfast, gifted the ancient bachelor with a German Shepherd puppy.

A transformation occurred in Mr. Johnson as Rex grew into adulthood. Loud voices caused the puppy to tremble, and so his new owner began to keep his tone gentle. On more than one occasion, Mr. Johnson beamed as his new dog performed the simple trick of holding his paw out for you to shake. I'm not sure I had witnessed a smile from the old man previously.

Mr. Johnson spent most days whittling spoons while arguing with other old-timers sitting on park benches. They compared each other's work and pointed out flaws. When voices rose in anger, Rex whined, and everyone stopped arguing.

One Sunday at lunch, Mr. Johnson brought up the pastor's sermon. "Do you think God gave us dogs to teach us about the fruits of the Spirit?"

"It's possible." Mama said.

"I've always wondered why Linda gave me Rex so I asked her." He paused and then said, "She told me the Holy Spirit prompted her to do it, and she didn't want to at first but decided to trust God."

Mom patted his hand. "It's a blessing when God allows us to be a part of His plan."

Mr. Johnson half smiled and said, "I hadn't realized how cantankerous I'd become."

"No one's perfect, and God knows exactly how to fix us," said Mom.

"The Lord surely knew I needed Rex," he agreed.

The same changes that took place in Mr. Johnson can take place in anyone's life once Jesus is welcomed in. That's when the void in a hidden chamber of the heart is filled and over-flows with the fruits of His Spirit.

The choice is ours. We can go the path alone or we can accept Jesus as our Master. Serving Him is easy because He fills our life with love, joy, peace, patience, kindness, goodness, faithfulness, gentleness, and self-control. The Father loves us and wants to abide within us. If you've wandered, the Shepherd will search for you and lead you back to the comfort of the flock, and He might even use a dog to do that.

Father, thank You for being my forever friend and please help me to demonstrate the fruit of Your Spirit to others. Amen.

The Trojan Dog

The Kingdom of Heaven can be illustrated by the story
of a king who prepared a great wedding feast for his son.
When the banquet was ready, he sent his servants to notify
those who were invited. But they all refused to come!

MATTHEW 22:2–3 NLT

Missy was a small Chihuahua mix stray of unknown origin that lived at my mother's home for a summer. Although Mom fed Missy on her front porch, Missy never made it inside Mom's house, that is until the week I visited with Kirby, my German Shepherd-Golden Retriever mix. Despite the great difference in their sizes, Kirby and Missy hit it off from the moment they met and became fast friends.

Oftentimes Missy waited at the front door for Kirby to come outside. When it was time for Kirby to go inside, Missy did everything she could to get in with her. One evening after Kirby played outside with Missy, I let Kirby in. Hiding beneath Kirby, and matching her step for step, strode Missy. Kirby seemed oblivious to the fact her friend snuck inside the house under her. While I thought the subterfuge was extremely brilliant and resourceful, my mother thought otherwise and Missy was promptly escorted out the door.

Thinking of the time Missy snuck inside Mom's house reminds me of the parable Jesus told about the wedding banquet a king threw for his son (Matthew 22:1–14). The king wanted everyone to attend. He sent out invitations, butchered the fattened cattle, and had everything ready. But those the king invited refused to come, so he sent out more invitations

111

to both the good and the bad. The king even provided special wedding clothes for all his guests. One man at the banquet, however, did not have on the special wedding clothes, and much like Missy, was thrown outside. He might have snuck inside, but he was not allowed to stay.

My mother had her rules: Kirby was allowed inside, Missy was not. I believe part of the reason Missy was not allowed inside was her small size. Mom's eyesight was failing by then, and having Missy underfoot could've led to an unexpected fall. Despite the rule, Missy tried to sneak in anyway.

God has His house rules, too. Although He invites all to come inside and enjoy the wedding banquet of His Son, we are only allowed inside according to God's rules. His rules state we must be clothed in Christ's robe of righteousness. Jesus Christ is the way, the truth, and the life. No one can come to the Father except through Him (John 14:6). We can't sneak in, but we can choose to receive the free gift—Christ's robe of righteousness—that gives us all access to God's house.

Father, thank You for Your invitation to come into Your house—
not because of who we are, or what we've done,
but because of who Jesus is and what He has done. Amen.

Come Back Here, Sweetie!

In your great mercy you did not put an end to them
or abandon them, for you are a gracious and merciful God.

NEHEMIAH 9:31 NIV

Joe had a black cocker spaniel named Sweetie—a dog that nobody wanted until Joe and his wife adopted her. But they quickly fell in love with their furry friend and had a hard time resisting her whenever she looked at them with her soulful eyes. The name they chose was appropriate because that dog truly was sweet.

And she was smart, sometimes too smart for her own good. Sweetie could sense when people were going to leave the house. If guests were there and someone started to leave, she'd stand near the door, and then when they opened it and weren't looking, she'd dart outside, race up the hill, and hide behind the trees.

Some days it was frustrating, especially if Joe was in a hurry and needed to get somewhere. He would call for her, patting his leg, "Come here, Sweetie! Come on!" But she'd played the game one time too many to fall for that. She would peek around the trees and thought nobody could see her, but she was quite visible.

Nothing worked. Joe chased her many times as he tried to win the dog vs. master challenge, but just as he would get to her and think he had finally caught her, Sweetie would slip out of his hands and dart away. He never won the battle.

And then Joe figured out what to do—something he would do many times after that. He hopped in the car and drove to the end of the driveway like he was leaving. Then he opened the door and called for her, and she ran to the car and jumped into the seat. Then Joe drove back up the driveway, retrieved Sweetie from the seat, and put her back into the house.

I wonder how many times I've done the same thing with God. He'd say, "Stay here with me where it's safe." But in my vaulted wisdom—just like that silly dog—I ran from Him. And then in shame, I hid from Him. Well, at least I *thought* I hid from Him.

But just as Joe could look up the hill to where most of Sweetie could be seen behind the tree branches, God knew exactly where I was. And just as Joe did what was necessary to retrieve Sweetie from the hill so he could put her back in the house where she'd be safe, God kept after me until I returned back to Him. I'm so grateful that He's a patient and loving God, that He never forsakes me even when I wander off. And I hope I'll be more sensitive to His voice next time He calls, "Come back here, Sweetie."

Father, thank You for always chasing after me
and bringing me back to You when I stray.
Help me to stay close to You. Amen.

Live to Give

Every good and perfect gift is from above, coming down
from the Father of the heavenly lights,
who does not change like shifting shadows.

JAMES 1:17 NIV

Is your dog on your Christmas list? Mine is. I love to give my Dachshund, Mollie Mae, all of the things she adores. Lately, she's been rather partial to a toy hedgehog that honks when you squeeze it, so I've stocked up on several of them since Miss Mollie is also quite gifted at tearing out "the honker" on those toys. I'll be placing the beloved hedgehogs in Mollie's doggie stocking so that she will have a very Merry Christmas alongside my human children.

Even when it's not the holiday season, I enjoy giving Mollie little surprises. Sometimes I'll go to two or three different stores until I find Mollie's favorite dog treats. I bet you do the same thing for your precious pup. I just love blessing my little Doxie diva. I can hardly wait to see her reaction when I pull her treats from the bag. She barks and howls and jumps on her hind legs with excitement, which always brings a smile to my face.

Just think, as much as we love to give our dogs the desires of their little hearts, it pales in comparison to how much our heavenly Father enjoys blessing us. Where do you think that desire to give unto others (even our canine companions) comes from? It comes from God. Matthew 7:11 (NIV) says, "If you, then, though you are evil, know how to give good gifts to your children, how much more will your Father in heaven give good gifts to those who ask him!"

God is the best present giver. He can hardly wait to give you good things. Every gorgeous sunset. Every beautiful rainbow. Every gentle rain. Every ocean breeze. Every good thing comes from God, and it pleases Him to give them to us. And don't forget, He already gave us the best gift—His son Jesus Christ—who died on the cross so that we might have eternal life. What a gift!

God loves to see us enjoying the blessings He sends our way. So, enjoy all of the gifts in your life today. Praise Him for your many blessings. By doing that, you are blessing the Father. Oh, and go ahead, and give your dog a special treat today too. Let the attitude of gratitude and the spirit of giving fill you up and overflow onto everyone you encounter.

Father, I appreciate all of the special gifts
that You give to me—I love how You love me, Lord!
Help me live to give. Amen.

The General

The LORD always keeps his promises;
he is gracious in all he does.

PSALM 145:13 NLT

My stop at Dollar General for paper goods one day turned into much more. In the parking lot, a mother and son held cardboard boxes teeming with puppies, pleading with customers to take one home for Christmas. I knew better than to take a closer look. We already had a dog, two cats, and a rabbit.

However, when asked if I wanted one, I responded, "Oh no, I couldn't. My husband would not be happy if I brought home another animal. Just let me hold one a minute, though." That tiny shivering pup nestled into the crook of my arm and buried his nose in my elbow, whimpering. Suddenly, the scheming side of me surfaced and I decided this little fellow would make the perfect Christmas present for my husband!

Our son dubbed him General since we found him at Dollar General, but the name fit remarkably well. Though never assertive or aggressive, General commanded our attention in subtle ways. When he needed to go out, he stood quietly by the door until someone noticed. When his water bowl was empty, he nudged it noisily with his nose until we refilled it. When one of us seemed sad, he nestled at our feet and emitted big sighs of sympathy. If my husband appeared stressed, General pressed against his knees as though to remind him to relax. They watched television together every night, the best of buds. General became such an integral part of our family that he soon accompanied us on vacations. That had never happened in our pet kingdom before. However, he proved such a good traveler, it was worth the bit of inconvenience required to take him along.

A Golden Retriever-yellow Lab mix, General looked dapper and cheery in his bright red winter jacket. He loved long walks on the Cottonwood Trail near our house and enjoyed meeting other "friends" along the way. Though shy of strangers, he seemed to attract the attention of all passersby who wanted to reach out and pet him. He made frequent visits to my mother-in-law in her assisted living facility, trotting obediently down the hallways and up to the side of her bed so she could pat his head. His ability to calm her restlessness generated tremendous gratitude on her part and ours.

At age eleven, General fought his last battle. We greatly miss him, but the memories of this precious pet also bring us quiet joy. And with the memories comes the reminder that the Lord always keeps His promises and He's gracious in all He does. He commands our attention with loving kindness, focuses our awareness and moves us to action, and brings us peace in His presence when we need it the most. May we have confidence in God's faithfulness, and like General, share love with all those on our path.

Lord, thank You for Your loving faithfulness. Amen.

King
of the Mountain

Let us not grow weary of doing good,
for in due season we will reap, if we do not give up.

GALATIANS 6:9 ESV

I remember Charlie as the perfect dog—sweet-tempered, loyal, protective. He never barked except when strangers approached his family, and we never kept him on a leash or in a fence because he never wandered away from us. He remained by my side when I was home.

When I went to school, he took up guard on the back patio, leaving only to follow my mother to the clothesline. Charlie would sprawl on the grass while she hung up sheets, so that she'd have to step over him. He would then trail her back to the house and wait for the appropriate treat. He loved scrambled eggs, and my mother could be quite the softy when it came to those big brown eyes.

A German Shepherd-Collie mix, Charlie was alert but calm, that is until the day the guy on the earth-moving machine arrived and began to dig up the lot next door. The owner planned to build a house, but Charlie considered that his territory. We had to keep him locked in the house to prevent him from charging the machine, attempting to block its progress. We tried to calm him, but Charlie wouldn't have it.

His fury made my dad take a second look at the lot. He talked to the neighbor on the other side of the lot, and together they made an offer on the property. The owner stopped work on the land, leaving a pile of dirt more than twenty feet high.

Charlie was in heaven. He'd sit on top of the mound, surveying his "kingdom," keeping watching on the neighborhood. Mostly it was a quiet place, although he did alert us to strangers who "stole" the garbage on Fridays. There was also that one slow traveling truck that turned out to be driven by someone who was, in fact, casing the houses for possible burglary. Charlie also convinced a man that his naïve, fourteen-year-old companion should not be approached.

Charlie appeared sweet and placid, but he never dropped his guard. His family was his first priority, and he never grew "weary of doing good." He set a standard, and we loved him unconditionally for it.

Throughout the Bible, we're instructed to stay alert for the enemy and to continually do good for our fellow believers (see Philippians 2:4; Galatians 6:2, 6, 9–10; Ephesians 4:32). Putting our faith into action, making the effort to uplift and care for all of God's children is an essential part of our calling to follow the ways of Jesus.

Lord, we love all Your creation and Your children.
Please guide us as we "stay on guard,"
caring for and encouraging others. Amen.

Our Deepest Longings

I opened my mouth wide and panted,
for I longed for your commandments.

PSALM 119:131 NASB

At just eight pounds, Cupcake looked like a ball of black and brown fur. So when that little ball of fluff chased after a playground ball that matched her size, it appeared as if two balls were rolling around on the floor, not just one.

My little Yorkie chased that ball with so much vigor she'd often completely drench herself in slobber. I'd try to figure out if she had worked up a sweat (do dogs sweat?) or if it was just saliva. I finally deduced it was the latter. That little dog panted so much she looked like she had stuck her head under a water hose.

Ferociously, she panted and ran after that ball—all across the floor, around furniture, and, on occasion, even down the stairs to the basement. She nearly dislocated her hip trying to keep up with the bouncy ball as it swiftly cleared the stairs. She kept panting and chasing until we took the ball away and made her stop. Often she seemed happy for the chase to end so that she could cool off and lap down a bowl of water.

I've never longed for something to the point of physically panting. My stomach's growled, my mouth has watered, and my brain has engaged in some ridiculous obsessions. Fear has caused me to sweat, but I've never wanted something so much that it caused me to pant.

That's a fierce longing. A heartfelt desire. The deepest type of yearning. The kind of drive I'm only supposed to have for God alone.

Dogs have such simple lives. Satisfaction rarely eludes them. They stick to the basics: food, water, a warm place to sleep, appropriate attention to special needs, and affection. Boom! That's it. The comprehensive list of what it takes to keep a dog content reads blissfully short. The opportunity to occasionally chase a toy ranks as a treat. Rarely fickle with their desires, dogs keep first things first.

Me, on the other hand. Oh my! The list of what I believe I need to find contentment morphs and grows daily. Foolishly, I think my idols will satisfy me. I haphazardly crave this and wish for that, my heart bouncing like Cupcake's rubber ball around those things that I hope will fill me. But my wanting remains. I misplace my hope.

I think of how the psalmist writes, "As a deer pants for flowing streams, so pants my soul for you, O God" (Psalm 42:1 ESV). How often do I fail to make Jesus who and what I long for the most? While I distract myself with other, lesser longings, I miss the joy that comes from panting for my Savior and yearning for His truth. When I make my primary longing for Him, only then will I find true and lasting contentment.

*Dear Lord, teach me to pant. Help me remember
that when my desire is for You alone,
I will always find satisfaction. Amen.*

Over the Fence

"If you love me, keep my commands."

JOHN 14:15 NIV

Pepsi was a Brittany Spaniel. Because we lived in town, Daddy fenced in a large part of our property for a dog pen. When Pepsi was small, he had no option but to stay inside his pen. But as he grew older and taller, he figured out several paths to freedom.

Pepsi loved sitting on his dog house. One day, he stood up on the dog house and realized he could leap from the roof over the top of the four-foot fence. Daddy moved the dog house farther away from the fence.

Pepsi tried to dig out of the pen at the corner. Daddy reinforced the fence by putting logs around the bottom and adding a few extra in the corner. He stacked several to make sure Pepsi couldn't move the logs. However, Pepsi saw stacked logs as another escape route. He walked up them like steps, then took a short hop to freedom over the fence. Daddy unstacked the logs to eliminate the "stairs."

Once that path to freedom was gone, Pepsi stayed in his pen, no doubt thinking about his next means of escape. After a few days, Daddy came down the steps and there was Pepsi, out of his pen again. Daddy put him back and went in the house to watch out the window. Pepsi sat at the gate until he heard the door close, went back to the lower corner of the fence, stood on the one remaining log, and "walked" up the chain link fence to freedom.

Next, Daddy put an electric fence on top of the existing chain link fence, with the motor in the garage. Once installed, Daddy had no more problems with his canine escape artist—or so we thought. After a few weeks of no escape attempts, Daddy decided to turn off the electric fence and conserve electricity, sure that Pepsi would see the wire and think it would still shock him. However, not too long after, my sister and I went outside to play and were greeted at the back door by none other than Pepsi! Apparently Pepsi's ears worked well. Daddy figured out Pepsi was listening for the motor hum before he tried his escape. From then on the motor was left on.

Pepsi was not unlike me. Sometimes I want to do things that are not the best for me. I refuse to accept parameters that keep me safe. I listen to God's direction but think I know a better way. Thank goodness He never gives up on trying to show me how to do the right thing! Do you ever want to do things that are not good for you? Do you need a fence to keep you separated from the temptations? God wants the best for us. He has given us boundaries because He loves us. All we have to do is look in His Word where He has provided us with clear direction. And it is our choice to follow His lead or hop the fence.

Lord, thank You for Your patience and loving instruction.
Help me to listen and obey. Amen.

Sweet Surrender

For as the heavens are higher than the earth,
so are My ways higher than your ways,
and My thoughts than your thoughts.

ISAIAH 55:9 NKJV

They overturn our trash cans, dig in our back yards, and jump onto our couches. They may even chew our good shoes and demolish the furniture. Even if our beloved dogs torture the neighbor's cat, we love them—despite their flaws. When it comes to our fur babies, we demonstrate extreme benevolence and mercy. Even when angry, we don't stop loving them.

Sadie, our Heinz 57 bird dog, drives us crazy with her incessant need to play tug of war. During walks, she pulls on the leash and refuses to drop the ball during a game of fetch. The tan and white mutt always tries to lure us into a tugging match.

Sadie's favorite item to tug is a short rope with thick knots on each end. Instead of retrieving it, she would rather try and wrestle that rope out of our hands. Good luck if you try and take it away. A gentle tug can quickly turn into a battle of wills, with Sadie pulling all the harder. When Sadie has the rope, it's nearly impossible to pull it away.

The dog's penchant for pulling always reminds me of summer camp where we played tug of war until our hands burned red and hot. The designated anchor—usually the biggest and strongest kid—would tie the rope around his waist and dig his heels into the ground.

Like Sadie's fondness for tug of war, we can refuse to hand over certain aspects of our lives to God. We may fight for our own way like we once played at summer camp, keeping our hands on the rope until callouses form and our hands throb, or until exhaustion sets in and our feet have dug deep ruts in the ground.

To be honest, I play tug of war with God when I constantly try to control my life. How often do I resist God and want to wander from the path where He leads? How many times does God need to call my name before I answer? Before I surrender?

Sometimes I resist God without even knowing it. My way seems right to me, but God's way seems foreign and upside down. I only learn to surrender to God's will with a lot of practice. When I start each day waving the white flag allowing God to bring in His perfect plan for my life, I taste the sweet communion that surrender brings. And on the days when I mess up big, God grants grace and forgiveness in abundance. God is merciful and benevolent, and His love never quits.

Lord, show me all the ways I'm battling against Your perfect plan so that I may release and relax in Your will. Amen.

Follow the Right Leader

My sheep listen to my voice;
I know them, and they follow me.

JOHN 10:27 NLT

Samantha, our Samoyed, was sneaky. She was also a persuasive leader. This combination not only resulted in trouble for her, but for Shadow, our German Shepherd-Labrador Retriever, as well. Although Shadow was not sneaky, he was a willing follower, and that often resulted in trouble for him.

During one blustery winter's day, our backyard gate blew open while Shadow and Samantha were outside. We didn't realize they were missing until some time after they escaped. When we saw the open gate and the dogs didn't come when called, my son and I began a search of the neighborhood. We checked with our neighbors. No one had seen them. Then we got into our car and slowly drove through the area calling and looking for the two runaways.

After an exhaustive, empty-handed search, we reluctantly returned home to wait. We knew Shadow would not leave the yard on his own. It didn't take much to figure out that when Samantha noticed the open gate, she seized the opportunity, and Shadow simply followed her lead.

After several long hours of waiting, one of our neighbors knocked on our front door. Standing on the porch beside him were Shadow and Samantha. From the look of the two dogs, I'd say wherever it was they'd gone off to, they'd run the entire way there and back. Shadow trusted Samantha and followed her. Unfortunately, Samantha wasn't always trustworthy. It took Shadow the rest of the day and evening to recover from their escapade through the neighborhood.

There are times we might follow others or times others might follow us. Either way, it is good to know whose voice we're listening to, where we're going, and to count the cost before we set out, making sure the person we're following is trustworthy. When we lead, we should lead according to God's direction. When we follow, we should follow those going in God's direction.

The opposite can also be true. When we allow peer pressure to cloud our judgment and blindly follow someone without thinking through what it might cost us, we could find ourselves lost and in trouble. When we compromise our values as leaders who follow Jesus and let integrity slide, we are in danger of hurting those who follow.

It doesn't matter if we are in a position to lead or in a position to follow. What matters is whose voice we listen to. We are called Jesus's sheep. Jesus said His sheep listen to His voice. They follow Him. The only way we will know His voice is to become so familiar with what He says in the Bible that there can be no mistaking it.

*Father, give me ears that listen to Your voice,
so I will follow You alone, and teach me to lead in such
a way that others will be drawn closer to You. Amen.*

Committed
Companion

*I love the LORD, because he has heard my voice
and my pleas for mercy. Because he inclined his ear to me,
therefore I will call on him as long as I live.*

PSALM 116:1-2 ESV

My Golden Retriever, Simon, and I arrived at the library early for his first session with a reluctant reader. A year earlier I'd recognized my dog's gentle nature made him the perfect candidate for a therapy dog.

During Simon's session with Bobby, I sat in the corner and watched the seven-year-old boy ignore the book in his lap while he stroked Simon's head. During the second session, the book lay on the floor and I started to intervene. However, as I approached the pair, I noticed Bobby wiping a tear from his cheek as he placed his head on Simon's shoulder.

Later I learned Bobby's foster parents were in the process of adopting him and that the sad boy had lived in twenty different foster homes. His new mom sighed. "Sometimes, he seems so forlorn. Maybe having a dog of his own will help." Bobby's parents checked out books about different dog breeds, and they asked me to help them select a dog at the shelter. I agreed, but suggested Bobby be allowed to choose his dog.

At the shelter, we toured a room full of puppies, but Bobby passed each one. "Don't you have an older dog?" He said.

"Of course," said the volunteer. "But wouldn't you rather have a puppy?"

"Not many people want older kids," Bobby chewed his nail.

"Right this way," the worker said.

Bobby looked at the barking dogs, and stopped in front of one who looked like he could be Simon's relative. Bobby stuck his fingers in the mesh cage, and the dog's wet nose gave a sniff. The worker looked in her folder and said, "His name is Simon, but you can rename him. His owner passed away."

Bobby's jaw dropped. "No way." Both boy and dog had bounces in their steps when they left the shelter. Now this happy child often asks me about my Simon and tells me about his.

When others let Bobby down and he needed someone he could trust, God sent him Simon, who had the patience to listen. Simon comforted without words because he listened with his heart. Jesus, too, will sit in the quiet and listen to our troubles without judgment or condemnation. No matter what we tell Him, He'll always love us. Others may let us down, but Jesus won't. He offers love and mercy—His free gift of grace. Just as Bobby searched out Simon, may we search out Jesus as our companion, comforter, and confidant.

Thank You, Lord, for hearing my prayers, especially when I lack the words to speak. Thank You for never letting me down, and for helping me forgive those who have. Amen.

Bridget and
the Bad Dog

*Don't be fooled . . . for "bad company
corrupts good character."*

1 CORINTHIANS 15:33 NLT

B ridget, a Sheltie-Golden Retriever mix, had the energy of
a toddler on a sugar high. We lived in a secluded, heav-
ily wooded area, with only a few houses nearby. Most of the
dogs knew each other, and all the kids played together. Bridget
would run circles around us, trying to herd us into a group.

And Bridget loved the woods. After she exhausted the kids
in the neighborhood, she made sure all the cats were treed and
the rabbits chased back into their burrows. Her golden brown
coat could be seen flashing through the woods, pausing only
when the squirrels vanished into the treetops. The only animals
she left alone were the skunks, and we suspected her wariness
came from personal experience. Bridget came to us as an adult,
having already survived any number of adventures.

Bridget had a happy spirit, and her tail remained set on
"wag furiously." She always seemed to be smiling, and her obedience was legendary. She stayed close, and quickly picked up
any "trick" my brother tried to teach her. She adored us and
we did her.

It was a time of innocence, when we all knew and trusted
each other. Then "Lady" moved into the neighborhood. Lady
had a white coat and a nose for trouble. Almost immediately
after her arrival at any neighbor's house, chickens would vanish

or garbage cans would be tipped over. She chased cars and growled at the neighborhood children. My father's warnings were immediate and severe. "Keep Bridget in the house or on a leash. That dog will corrupt every dog she's around." We tried, much to Bridget's dismay.

Our neighbor tried to break Lady of her bad habits, and built her a chain-link enclosure which she dug under and climbed over. Lady finally disappeared into the woods, and she thwarted all attempts to capture her. My father built a tall, wooden fence in an attempt to keep Bridget safe, but she chewed through one of the planks and wiggled free. A few days later, we saw her with Lady, both carrying chickens. They made their home in the woods and we were never able to retrieve them. Our lovely Bridget had been forever changed.

It was a lesson I never forgot, and the wisdom of Scripture emphasizes this. Not only will we be known by the company we keep, but we can easily be changed by them (see Proverbs 13:20; 22:24–25). While love and goodness can also be influential, we have to be careful; evil is powerful and can show up where we least expect it (1 Peter 5:8). Keeping our eyes on the ways of the Lord is vital. Only when we focus on Him can we be a guide for others.

Lord, help me keep my eyes on You,
and help me be an example to others, showing that following
Your Word is filled with blessings and love. Amen.

Disciplined Rewards

Delight yourself also in the LORD,
and He shall give you the desires of your heart.

PSALM 37:4 NKJV

I'd spent the morning doing back-breaking labor, using clippers and scissors to maintain my beautiful Airedale Terrier pup. Both of us were entitled to a favorite reward for our efforts. Pearl flashed her beautiful brown eyes, shaded under long lashes and amber fluffy brows, to signal her greatest desire. "Throw the ball and I'll make you proud!" she seemed to say.

I took the bait. Twenty throws into our game, I felt satisfied and safe. My clean, twenty-month-old girl should be finished with her play and I anticipated a well-earned rest. A vision of a lovely cup of tea soon shattered when she bolted and made haste to her favorite spot of iniquity. The horse barn offers much in the line of doggie temptation, all of which are harmful to her health and appearance.

She did it to me again. I reminded myself that puppies will challenge their owners until they learn who their pack leader is. A problem with Airedales is that they learn quickly but spend the rest of their lives deciding if they will comply.

After a brief roll in something smelly, she ran to the unraked paddock. Piles of temptations rose before her and she gleefully tossed them about, stopping briefly to inhale before she chewed. The lure of manure proved more enticing than fifty-dollar-a-bag dog food. Now filthy and infested, my formerly clean baby shot me a few glances of euphoric contentment before she ran wildly in circles around and under the horses. I feared she'd be kicked or trampled but the pup remained oblivious.

The only way to arrest the temptation was to dangle something more tempting. I started the truck, popped the horn a few times, and moved toward the driveway. Pearl loves to ride and flew in my direction, tongue dangling over a tan beard now crusty brown, and hopped into the open cab door. Gotcha! I lead her, panting and filthy, back to the dog shower. With hot tea on the horizon, I prayed she wouldn't require another all-night potty break like the last episode.

Trying to explain to Pearl the benefits of obedience is about the same as the Lord enlightening me in my hard-of-hearing times. When I learn what He wants and comply, life is so much less complicated, cleaner, healthier, and richer. If I accept His desires as my own, the rewards are boundless without chastisement.

For now, Pearl remains grounded with more training to do. She has yet to learn what I have: The Master will offer greater blessings as I delight in Him.

Lord, teach me to be trusted off-leash
and receive Your immeasurable rewards. Amen.

Picking
the Right Fight

For our struggle is not against flesh and blood,
but against the rulers, against the authorities,
against the powers of this dark world and against
the spiritual forces of evil in the heavenly realms.

EPHESIANS 6:12 NIV

Blondie was my first dog. I told my parents I didn't want a mutt, but they convinced me a "mixed" dog would be okay. When one of my father's coworker's dogs had puppies, he took me to choose one from the litter. A Beagle-Dachshund mix, Blondie was a wriggling ball of energy with fur about the same shade as my white-blond hair.

Blondie was a good first dog for a child, but she wasn't very bright. She was prone to getting herself into scrapes. We had a hive of fat, lazy carpenter bees living in the honeysuckle along our back fence. They didn't bother us, and we didn't bother them. Blondie was also usually content to leave them alone— at least until my father started up the lawnmower. As soon as he pulled the cord and revved the engine, Blondie would run over to the beehive and start barking and snapping at the nest, jumping and yelping until one of the bees started chasing her. At that point, Blondie bolted for my father, the bee flying close behind. My father started carrying a tennis racket so he could swat the bees when Blondie came yelping for him to save her.

The problem wasn't the mower, it was Blondie picking the wrong fight. Those bees weren't bothering her—at least not until she started snapping at them. When she started harassing the bees, that's when the trouble began.

I laughed at Blondie's silliness, but sometimes I do the same thing. I pick the wrong fights—taking up offense where none was meant, blowing molehills into mountains, and nagging at minor problems until they fester into major sores. And in the process I blind myself to the real battle: the spiritual battle that wages in the heavens, unseen but still very real. I need to remember who my real enemy is.

My real enemy is not the coworker I can't stand, the slow-as-molasses cashier, or the person who sees the world through different political lenses than I do. My struggle is against the spiritual forces and powers in rebellion against God who want to destroy my witness and my walk. The problems and struggles I face are only symptoms of a greater struggle in which prayer is my greatest weapon and Christ has already won the victory.

Wasting our time on the wrong fight is as pointless as a dog trying to eat bees—we only wind up getting stung. So today I remember the real battle. I choose to pick the right fight, and fight it with prayer.

Lord, remind me who my enemy really is,
and that You are victorious and help me
fight my battles with prayer. Amen.

Taming Swiper

Blessed is the one who trusts in the LORD,
whose confidence is in him.

JEREMIAH 17:7 NIV

Early one morning, I went outside to feed my animals and to do some chores when I heard something down the street. Soon a little dog, barking like crazy, came running up my driveway. I hadn't seen this dog before—a Pug mix—and he was quite a sight: fuzzy, with short legs and a severe underbite. To be honest, he was one of the ugliest dogs I have ever seen, but I was drawn to him anyway. I offered my hand in an effort to get to know him, but he refused. The more I tried to approach him, the more he resisted. As I did my chores, he followed me around, still barking and treating me like an outsider in my own yard.

That afternoon, I did some checking and discovered the dog belonged to the family who had just moved in down the street. The children in the family had named him Swiper, after the fox character from the television show *Dora the Explorer*. He seemed to be as sly as a fox, visiting every morning but dodging my attempts to touch him.

For the next month, I was determined to befriend Swiper. I threw him dog treats; he came close enough to snatch them and then run away. One day I decided to sit on my front steps, on his level, for our morning encounter. He snapped up his dog biscuit and ran back down the street toward his house. We followed this routine for several days, and gradually he came closer. He soon stopped to sniff my hand, and from that point he took "baby steps" in getting to know me. Eventually Swiper allowed me to touch him, and after a while I was able to pet him on the head. Our routine changed, as he would meet me for his treat and some attention as I tended my pets. He still followed me but no longer barked like I was his enemy. With patience, I earned Swiper's trust.

When I first believed in God, trusting Him did not come naturally to me. I am an only child and have always been self-sufficient—a take-charge person, moving forward in my own strength. Trust this Someone with the details of life? Not me. I could take care of myself. I was as stubborn as Swiper, keeping my distance while doing life my way. Just as I had treats for Swiper, God had good things planned for me, but I wanted to do things my way. Little by little, God showed me that He has my best interests in mind, and that trust comes through cultivating a relationship with Him. The closer I get to God the more I realize I can trust Him, kind of like my friendship with that rowdy little dog.

Lord, day by day, keep teaching me
to trust You with everything. Amen.

A Fierce Protector

*The Lord is faithful, and He will strengthen
and protect you from the evil one.*

2 THESSALONIANS 3:3 NASB

My son and daughter-in-law had a black Lab named Daisy. She was gorgeous, with sleek fur and brown eyes that melted your heart. Daisy was one of the sweetest dogs I've ever met. She was a lover, gentle natured, and affectionate to all who knew her.

I worried about how she would adapt when my daughter-in-law became pregnant. Their furry friend had been the darling of the house, and now a tiny newcomer would soon arrive, taking the attention from Daisy, and adding activity and noise to their once peaceful environment.

But my worries were in vain, because from the moment Jack made his entrance into their home, Daisy was his biggest admirer. She loved that little guy. She would hover in concern whenever he cried, and then she would plop down as close as she could get to him.

As the months went by and Jack began walking, Daisy's patience amazed me as she became another toy for her little buddy. Jack sat on her, used her for a backrest, placed items on her, and we even found him walking across Daisy a time or two. But his furry buddy never snapped at him. The love between the two was evident and touching.

I stayed with Jack one day each week while his mama worked, and that's when I saw another side of Daisy. On one memorable afternoon as Jack and I sat on the couch reading books, Daisy lurched to her feet from where she'd been sleeping on the floor in front of us. The ruff on her back stood on end, and a deep guttural growl rumbled from her. My heart almost jumped from my chest it scared me so badly. Then she started barking furiously as she took a protective stance between Jack and the danger she perceived at the door.

It was just the mailman waiting for a signature for a package, but I was so touched by Jack's fierce protector. There was no doubt in my mind that Daisy would have fought to the death for this little boy who she loved so much.

That reminds me so much of my relationship with God. I'm blown away by how loving He is with me, how He's so patient whenever I hurt Him or when I mess up. It boggles my mind that He wants to spend time with me, and I love that I can feel His presence wherever I am. And yet, this gentle and loving God is also my fierce protector, and nothing, *nothing*, can harm me unless it comes through Him first. It's impossible to be any safer than when we're with someone who is willing to give His life for us.

Father, thank You for being my protector
and for the peace that brings. Amen.

Take the Plunge

This is my command—be strong and courageous!
Do not be afraid or discouraged.
For the LORD your God is with you wherever you go.

JOSHUA 1:9 NLT

English Springer Spaniels are known for their love of water and will plunge into any watery habitat given the chance. However, my dog of the same breed hesitated to even get his paws wet. No matter how much I encouraged him.

One hot July day while out for a walk, we came to a shallow, babbling brook. Children splashed happily in the gentle running water, taking the chance to cool off from the sultry weather. I decided this was the ideal opportunity to cure my Springer's fear of water once and for all. I rolled up my jeans, slipped off my sneakers and socks, and stepped into the ankle-deep stream. "Come on," I coaxed, slapping my thigh in an effort to persuade my dog to follow me.

Fink stood on the grassy bank, whining. He stepped forward, making me believe he would take the plunge. Then he backed up, thinking better of it. He wanted to obey the command of his mistress, yet fear won over.

I waited, continually calling his name. Eventually, he stepped gingerly into the water. He waded over toward me until he stood by my side. I patted his head. "Good boy," I said in soothing tones, "not so bad after all, huh?"

God commanded Joshua to cross the Jordan River and lead the people into the land God had promised them. The people didn't have a fear of water; however, they had good reason to be frightened of the people who inhabited the land on the other side of the river. God told Joshua not to be afraid. He could be courageous because God would be with him.

It is the same for us. Sometimes God leads us to places we don't want to go. No matter what we face, God commands us to be strong and courageous. "Come and join me," He encourages, but like my dog we stand on the bank too scared to follow. Just as God was with Joshua, He will be with us. Jesus also instructs us to follow Him. He assures us He would never leave us. Even though Jesus returned to heaven, we are not alone. We have God's Spirit to give us strength. There is no need to be fearful.

The following summer, my husband and I took our dog to the beach. Before we could stop him, he tore across the sand toward the sea. He splashed through the shallows into the breaking waves and began swimming—straight out to sea!

Where is God leading that you are reluctant to go? Where is the Lord asking you to step out for Him? Be brave. Soon you could be amazing others with your courage.

Dear Lord, help me not to be afraid to follow
where You are leading.
Instead, give me the courage to do Your will. Amen.

God Looks
at the Heart

*GOD told Samuel, "Looks aren't everything.
Don't be impressed with his looks and stature.
I've already eliminated him. GOD judges persons differently
than humans do. Men and women look at the face;
GOD looks into the heart."*

1 SAMUEL 16:7 MSG

Shang was the runt of his litter and not worth keeping. At least that's what my sister, who is a dog breeder, said. My friend Marie had little hope for the small German Shepherd puppy when he was born. Because my older sister doubted she would be able to sell Shang, Marie gave me her castoff. And at twelve years old, boy, was I pleased!

I loved this puppy and he loved me back. He was perfect. Shang followed me around and protected me from anyone or anything that threatened me. That included my brother, which made me especially happy.

Throughout Shang's first year he proved Marie wrong in her assessment of his potential. Shang grew to over 100 pounds, and when he stood on his hind legs and placed his paws on my shoulders, he could look me in the eye. If Shang was the runt, I couldn't imagine how big he would've been if he was "normal."

Marie made the same error a lot of us do. We look at someone and judge their potential based on what they look like. Judging by the clothes they wear, the color of their skin, where they live, or how much money they have, we often write off people as "runts" without taking the time to get to know who they really are. Fortunately for us, that's not how God judges.

When God sent the prophet Samuel to Bethlehem to the house of Jesse, he discovered that God looks at the heart, not outward appearances. Samuel was sent to anoint Israel's future king. When he saw how handsome Jesse's sons were, he thought surely one of them was God's chosen. But they weren't. God's chosen, David, was actually out in the fields tending sheep, but no one even bothered to included him in the prophet's selection process. That's how little David's father thought of his runt.

Because I didn't judge by appearances, I didn't base Shang's worth on what he looked like when he first came into my life. Nor did I base his worth on another's assessment of his potential. It wouldn't have matter to me if Shang remained small. I still would have loved him and cared for him because he loved and protected me with his life.

God doesn't measure our worth based on what we look like. It's what's inside our heart that counts. Are we passionate for Christ? Do we desire God above all else? Do we trust Him and gladly follow His commands? Those are the things God looks at. Outward appearances don't fool God. He knows what we're really like.

Father, thank You for looking at my heart,
and judging me by Your perfect standard—Christ. Amen.

How to Stop
a Dog Fight

The roving band of stray dogs had prowled the neighborhood for weeks, and despite all efforts, no one could catch them. They tormented the other animals, spilled garbage cans, stole food, and dug holes in manicured lawns. Whenever they could start a fight, they did.

Sammy and Boots watched this from behind their backyard fence, apparently confident they were safe. And whenever the pack came around, they retreated to the patio.

These two were unlikely friends. Sammy, at ten weeks and eighteen pounds, scampered about with trips and stumbles, his lanky German Shepherd legs not quite under control. The runt of the litter, Sammy was less dog than mobile stuffed animal.

Boots could not have been more opposite. Eight years old, Boots was a majestic blend of Maine coon cat and Norwegian forest cat. Gray and black with white feet, Boots stood twenty-two inches tall, was thirty-eight inches nose to tail, and weighed twice what Sammy did. No one touched Boots without her permission, which she seldom gave. She moved slowly, with a regal air. No one dared question her rule over the house.

So Sammy's new owners weren't sure how Boots would welcome the clumsy puppy. They expected resistance, possibly violence. Sammy, however, seemed to appeal to Boots's maternal side, which had never been apparent before. She would lie next to him as he slept; sometimes *on* him if he had a nightmare, to comfort him. She watched him play from a distance, an aloof but doting mother. Aloof, that is, until the day the roaming pack of dogs found a gap in Sammy's fence.

The pack immediately made a target out of the young puppy, burying him beneath a growling mass of fur. Before Sammy's owner could react, a streak of gray and black flashed from the house, plowing into the fray. Dogs scattered in every direction as the cat's claws and teeth wreaked havoc. With the fight halted, Boots stood boldly next to her shivering friend, head up, shoulders square, tail proclaiming a warning dare.

Sammy was terrified but only bruised. The pack had suffered far more. They left the neighborhood, never to return. They had looked for trouble and found much more than they bargained for when they had stirred a calm presence into action.

Quarrelsome people are often like those dogs. They want to stir up trouble, whether in their neighborhood, church, or their own families. Those who remain calm, however, tend to see a "bigger picture," and can bring calm in their own determined way, waiting and making clear, decisive choices.

Throughout Scripture we're told to avoid arguments and strife (see Proverbs 20:3; Romans 14:1–23; 2 Timothy 2:23; Titus 3:9–11), but when quarrels happen, we are to take decisive action to end them.

Lord, help me avoid disagreements and division.
Show me, instead, a clear way to calm and peace,
following only Your way. Amen.

The Gift of Faith

She who is truly a widow, left all alone, has set her hope on God and continues in supplication and prayers night and day.

1 TIMOTHY 5:5 ESV

Sugar, an overweight miniature Poodle, looked like a jumbo marshmallow on four stick legs. Mrs. Ruth, her mistress, retired when her arthritis made it impossible to work. Her husband had died in an auto accident and she had one son who served in the military and lived in Japan. In those days, there was no internet and phone calls were a luxury Mrs. Ruth could not afford.

As a twelve-year-old, I'd roll my eyes when Mom said, "Let's stop and visit Ruth for a minute." The minute always turned into an hour or more. We would amble into the den where the chubby dog would jump into her mistress's lap and Mrs. Ruth would arrange her arthritic hands under Sugar's tummy where the warmth relieved the pain. Sometimes Sugar laid across Mrs. Ruth slippers. "Sugar knows just where I need her most," Mrs. Ruth said.

Often, Mrs. Ruth asked me to take Sugar outside to play. She'd only play for a few minutes, and then she'd race to the door and start howling. When we returned inside, the fat white fluff would run and lick Mrs. Ruth's face and hands. One might think they'd been separated for days instead of minutes.

At last, we'd say our goodbyes and Mom would say, "Pick up the phone and call anytime."

"Don't worry about me," Mrs. Ruth would say. "Sugar and the Lord keep me company."

It's only now as I am close to Mrs. Ruth's age that I consider her strong faith in God. She was "like a tree planted by water, that sends out its roots by the stream," as described in Jeremiah 17:8 (ESV). Never did I hear her complain of being lonely, and she accepted her illness as part of God's plan for her. She even called it a blessing because it allowed her to spend more time with the Lord. She found God's guidance in everything, even her arthritis and solitude.

How often do we only see our trials and struggles without realizing that God can use them to bless us or bless others. While I saw Mrs. Ruth as a lonely neighbor, she was a friend and mentor to my mother who needed her wisdom as she tried to raise her family. And, Sugar was the perfect representation of God's ceaseless affection and desire to love us and comfort us always. The synergy in this relationship was not a coincidence—God planned this in Mrs. Ruth's life.

He plans this in our lives too. I pray I will be more aware of how God works in my life through other people and even pets, and to not only enjoy the blessings of it, but also find my faith strengthened because of it.

Thank You, Father, for placing men and women of faith
in my life who have demonstrated joy
even during adversity. Amen.

The Guilty Dog

There is therefore now no condemnation
for those who are in Christ Jesus.

ROMANS 8:1 ESV

When Mali came home, he immediately saw evidence of a crime. The empty kitty treats bag lay open on the floor. Someone had taken a huge bite right out of its side. It didn't take Mali long to discover the culprit. Denver, a yellow Labrador Retriever, sat in a corner, wagging his tail nervously while flashing a squinty-eyed "snarl of guilt." A video of that adorable squint/snarl set the Internet aflame and earned the Labrador Retriever the moniker of "the guilty dog."

Denver kept getting into trouble, too. He ate crayons, wriggled his way into a bag of Doritos, demolished Christmas tree ornaments, and refused to take his medicine. When confronted with each sin, the dog always looked guilty, flashing the hilarious face. How can anyone stay mad at that?

While some dogs are sneakier than others and don't show any signs of guilt, many dogs, just like Denver, have their own version of the guilty face. These dogs might lower their head or lay their ears back. Or maybe they hide their face in shame, covering their eyes with their paws. But whether our dogs experience the complex emotions of guilt and shame or if they only react to our body language and tone of voice, it doesn't change the fact that we almost always forgive their indiscretions.

Our mercy for our pets mirrors the love and mercy of our heavenly Father. He is patient with us and altogether kind, despite our wanderings and missteps. He helps us make amends and continues His steadfast care of us. "The LORD is like a father to his children, tender and compassionate to those who fear him. For he knows how weak we are; he remembers we are only dust" (Psalm 103:13–14 NLT).

God knows, however, that fear is our default position. He understands that if we don't turn to Him to find forgiveness, guilt turns into poisonous condemnation. That's why His Word reminds us not to succumb to it—we now have no condemnation. When Jesus hung on the cross, He bore our sin, guilt, and shame. Our salvation includes total freedom from guilt and shame. We can accept God's complete forgiveness and rest in God's love and grace.

In Denver's case, it never took long for him to accept the forgiveness of his master and curl up beside him, resting his head in his lap. We humans have so much to learn from Denver. The ugly feelings of guilt and shame often send us hiding from God, not drawing us near to Him. In our moments of sin, however, God wants to forgive and shower His love and grace upon us. He invites His children to draw near for an embrace so He can tenderly whisper His love to us.

Lord, guard us against holding on to our condemnation,
and teach us to always draw near to You
for forgiveness and words of love. Amen.

Not What I Asked For

Stop judging by mere appearances,
but instead judge correctly.

JOHN 7:24 NIV

For several years, I told my father I wanted a Dachshund puppy for Christmas, partially because I loved the smooth brown hair of my friend's Dachshund, Felix. I had chosen the name Heidi for the cute female dog I envisioned.

When December arrived again, I pursued my campaign for Heidi at full speed. I even cut pictures of Dachshunds from my mother's magazines and placed them throughout the house. Unfortunately, Daddy was adamant about not having a dog. Undeterred, I accelerated my plan to persuade him by promising to feed, walk, and bathe Heidi. I also enlisted my mother to help soften Daddy's heart toward buying me a pet. Still, Daddy seemed to turn a deaf ear to my pleas.

As Christmas drew closer, I asked to visit Santa at the department store downtown as my backup plan, wanting Daddy to accompany me when I gave my list to jolly ole St. Nick. As I sat on Santa's lap, I pleaded my case for a puppy. Santa said he would do his best to answer my request. My talk with Santa seemed to help Daddy realize how much I wanted a dog.

To underscore the seriousness of my desire, I also asked to visit the pet store when we went into town. I wrote down the name, product number, and description of each item I thought would best suit Heidi. Remembering my friend's Dachshund, I picked out a pretty orange sweater that would compliment

Heidi's brown hair. I wanted my stocking to be filled with gifts for Heidi instead of the usual trinkets I received for myself.

When I went to bed on Christmas Eve, I was sure the next morning I would be awakened by a sweet woof.

On Christmas Day, my eyes popped open, and I ran to the tree ready to embrace my puppy. Indeed, there was a puppy asleep under the green boughs, but not the sleek brown Dachshund I had anticipated. Had Santa got the letters from some other child who wanted a dog mixed up with mine?

When Daddy brought the tricolored, long-haired dog to me, she greeted me with kisses of joy. Seeing my disappointment, Daddy explained that the puppy was a variation of the breed. He then placed the wiggly bundle in my arms, and I immediately fell in love with her, even though she did not remotely resemble what I had asked for.

Narrowing my perspective and blinding myself to other possibilities slowed down my ability to open up my heart and welcome my new pet. I've learned since then to look beyond "mere appearances" and to "judge correctly" what or who God has placed in my life. When we focus on the inner beauty of someone as He does, we deliver grace and love to all alike which brings glory to God.

Lord, help me see others as You do,
beautiful children of my heavenly Father. Amen.

Choices

Do you not know that your bodies are temples of the Holy Spirit,
who is in you, whom you have received from God?
You are not your own; you were bought at a price.
Therefore honor God with your bodies.

1 CORINTHIANS 6:19-20 NIV

This morning I gave Moose—my eleven pound, chocolate brown, Yorki-Poo—a bath in the kitchen sink. He tolerates his bath well, even though his brown eyes seem to communicate, "I can't believe you are doing this to me." After his bath, he runs like crazy, around and around.

Other than shredding a tissue occasionally on the floor, he's a pretty perfect pup. Except—well, this is kind of gross—but you know animals can do strange things. We live in the woods with lots of critters including deer, raccoons, skunks, and ground hogs. Okay, here's the gross part. My sweet, brown puppy will find a pile of fresh poo and roll around in it. Eww! That drives me crazy! And that is exactly what he did right after his bath.

Sometimes I wonder if he does this to get rid of the clean smell or if this is some form of rebellion, like "Stop manhandling me! Enough with the baths!" Who knows? Then an epiphany emerged, "I wonder if this is how God feels about me when I roll around in some routine sin of mine?"

For example, I struggle with gluttony. I know what to eat and proper proportions, but bring out the sweets and I lose my willpower. So after I eat the third cookie, does God close His eyes, shake His head, throw His hands in the air and say, "Oh, my dear, you know better. Why do you do that to yourself?"

That's exactly what I say to Moose rolling in the poo and to myself as I reach for the fourth cookie. I'm aware that eating sweets has no bearing on my salvation or God's love for me. But I sense the Holy Spirit disappointed in my choices. After all, my body is a gift from God to house the Holy Spirit. And the purchase price couldn't have been higher—the ultimate sacrifice of His perfect Son.

I want to live my life in a manner that puts a smile on His face, not in a manner that causes Him to shake His head. And since non-believers are watching me, I want to be an example of His light in a dark world. Now, I can't stop Moose from rolling in poo, but I do have control over my choices, especially when I know they don't align with God's will for me. Knowing that God does not require me to do all this in my own strength—He provides His strength whenever I ask for it—I can have the confidence to make choices that put a smile on His face.

Father, please help me to be mindful of Your will for my life and to make the right choices. Amen.

When Lightning Strikes

When I am afraid, I will put my trust in you.

PSALM 56:3 NLT

From the beginning, Polly showed no fear. She tumbled out of her litter, a ball of fluff seeking adventures. A white German Shepherd, she quickly left her brothers and sisters behind, begging to be picked up and cuddled.

A retirement gift for my father, Polly bonded instantaneously with him, and they were seldom apart after that. She stayed by his side in the garden and went for long rides in his truck. Polly loved being outside, especially in the rain, and many a storm moved through with my father watching from the porch as she gallivanted in the showers. If thunder and lightning showed up, he moved them into the garage. Polly pouted, but she trusted him, and would lie under his chair, tail thumping lazily on the concrete.

Because Polly couldn't go everywhere with him, my father built her a large enclosure near a shady tree and with a comfy house. It was her safe space, and sometimes she'd stand on the roof of the house, watching the world.

Then came the Sunday when a furious thunderstorm moved through while Mother and Daddy were at church, turning a beautiful sunny day into a nightmare. When they got home, he hurried toward the garden, where he found Polly huddled, shivering, in the back of her house. A neighbor told him later that lightning had struck a tree in the woods nearby. The current had apparently traveled along the ground.

Several hours passed before Polly stopped quivering in fear. My father sat on the floor with her in his arms, speaking softly, reassuring her. For the next two days, he did nothing but comfort her. She emerged from her fear, and seemed like the "normal" Polly—until the next thunderstorm.

The fear returned, and my father again wrapped his arms around her, comforting her until she calmed down. So it was for the rest of her life. The fear gripped her, but she always found solace and peace with my father.

How like our heavenly Father! Fear creeps up on us when we least expect it, catching us unaware and threatening to freeze and cripple us. No matter how much we trust the Lord, fear is a lurking beast.

God knows this, which is why He promises throughout Scripture that He will never leave us. "Don't be afraid, for I am with you. Don't be discouraged, for I am your God. I will strengthen you and help you. I will hold you up with my victorious right hand" (Isaiah 41:10 NLT).

We can always turn to Him for comfort. And He will always be there.

Father, thank You for holding me close, for never leaving me.
You are always there, waiting to comfort me. Amen.

Reality Check

My soul breaks with longing
for Your judgments at all times.

PSALM 119:20 NKJV

His arrival had been highly anticipated. The breeder placed Winston in my arms with a smile. "This is going to be a good one." After a ten-year stretch of caring for two dogs with long-term chronic illness, this healthy new Airedale Terrier pup came with a guarantee.

He displayed outstanding intelligence and willingness to obey. Anticipated success grew daily as we worked through basic commands, achieving perfection by the end of the first month. The uncanny image of his tiny body in a sit, stay, or roll-over position remains a most treasured memory. Leash adaptation came easily and, fueled by his developing strength and puppy enthusiasm, we developed into a capable, athletic team. We walked together every day, enjoying pastoral views and frequent sightings of deer and wild turkeys. I found it amazing that he responded to my commands to restrain, because he longed to chase.

After forty years of dog ownership, I had never owned a more intelligent, affectionate, obedient, or loving animal. Wonderful Winnie became a well-earned nickname.

I was blinded by his inherent perfection, for occasions still came when a few errors in his judgment occurred. He ate an entire bag of uncooked rice and ran up and down the stairs to get outside to eliminate. I chased him, dodging the involuntary expulsion, and forgot the incident after the stairway was sanitized.

Another time I was distracted by the doorbell. I returned to the stove where two loaves of bread dough had been rising and found the pans empty. After a call to the vet, administration of hydrogen peroxide solution to induce vomiting, and multiple trips outside throughout the remainder of the day, I again called him my good boy. As evening came, I forgave completely and put the day behind me.

He succumbed repeatedly to remnant food odors on grocery bags, and consumed a whole bottle of fish oil and an entire bag of cookies with Olympic prowess. Displaying an uncanny agility to lengthen his reach across the counter, he could snatch a sticky note off the backsplash behind the toaster.

He never destroyed belongings or bit anyone. Except for the rice incident, he continued as king of the housebroken. Eventually, reality came calling. I downgraded his stellar rating, realizing he was the one most affected by his own sins.

I am the same way. Successful in avoiding most sins my own breed has been found guilty of, I've succumbed to some appetites that have proved self-destructive. Within the adjusted assessment of my wonderful dog, I clearly saw myself in him. When I long to be restored in God's approval, the Lord meets me where I am, cleans me up and lifts me up, and calls me His child.

*Lord, help me to not be tempted by the cookies
out of reach so I can serve You in obedience. Amen.*

An Intentional Bump

*They do not fear bad news; they confidently trust
the Lord to care for them.*

PSALM 112:7 NLT

The first year I attended the Iditarod Sled Dog Race Conference for Teachers in Anchorage, Alaska, I learned that if at any time the sled dogs are unable to continue along the 1,049-mile route across the Alaska frontier from Anchorage to Nome, they are flown back to Anchorage by the Iditarod Air Force.

"Finney" (Andrea Aufder Heyde), the original Teacher on the Trail, told of an airplane ride she and several of the Iditarod dogs took from a remote checkpoint to Anchorage, Alaska. During Finney's flight back to Anchorage, the dogs became rather boisterous, and the pilot wished to quiet their howling. Without a word, the pilot pulled the plane's engine and the airplane dropped like a boulder. If you've ever experienced a turbulent plane ride, you get the idea. When that sudden drop happened, Finney said not one peep was heard for the remainder of the flight from any passenger on board the plane— four-footed, or two.

For those of us seated in the room the story was humorous. We could laugh because we weren't the ones in that airplane when it dropped altitude while flying over the remote frozen expanse of western Alaska.

When I recall this story, it causes me to think of the times God pulls the engine in our lives, and it feels like the bottom of our world has fallen out from under us. We plunge into a free fall, not knowing when, or if, we'll land safely. And if we do make it through the landing, where will we be, and in what kind of condition?

The Iditarod Air Force pilot on that flight needed the dogs' attention. He needed them to hush up, quit complaining, and trust him to deliver them safely back to Anchorage into the care of those waiting for them. The pilot knew explaining things to the dogs was useless. He knew he had to act. It was up to him to do something to grab their attention immediately, and it appears he knew exactly how to do that.

When God pulls the engine in our life, the jolt throws us off balance and sends us into a free fall. Just as the pilot pulled the airplane's engine to get the dogs' attention, God uses intentional bumps to do the same with us. Those bumps are a time for us to be still and listen to God's voice as He reminds us He is in control. He wants us to trust that He'll take care of us, and believe He'll deliver us safely to our destination.

Father, when I hit turbulence and the bottom seems
to have fallen out of my life, remind me You are in control
and this is Your way of getting my attention
and keeping my eyes fixed on You. Amen.

Waiting for Love

*Beloved, let us love one another, for love is from God,
and whoever loves has been born of God and knows God.*

I JOHN 4:7 ESV

Danny loves dogs and he missed having one of his own, but with his work schedule he knew he couldn't adequately care for a dog with the time and love it deserved. When his brother needed someone to keep his German Shepherd for a while, Danny was happy to do it, soaking in those moments of dog bliss as he petted and loved on the dog.

He missed his furry buddy when he had to go back home. So you can understand why a discovery Danny made one morning filled his heart with joy. While walking through the neighborhood, he discovered that a family with three kids had just adopted a six-month-old German Shepherd, a puppy that played in their fenced-in front yard. They had named him Crosby.

When the puppy saw Danny walking down the street, he ran over to him, his tail wagging in a friendly greeting. Danny stopped to pet him, and then as Danny started back on his stroll, the puppy walked down the fence line for Danny to keep petting him. Crosby was in doggie heaven as Danny rubbed his belly, under his chin, and behind his ears. It was instant love for both man and dog.

One only had to look at the furry bundle's paws to see that he was going to be a big dog. Danny later discovered that the owner had bought Crosby from people that sold dogs to the police department, so they were bred larger. The result was a German Shepherd with beautiful colors and lots of black markings on his back.

As the weeks and months went by, the two continued their daily visits. Crosby got to where he recognized Danny's steps when he walked down the sidewalk, and he'd come running out when he heard him. He'd jump up on the fence almost like he was trying to hug Danny. Sometimes Danny would pretend he didn't see the dog. Crosby would walk down the fence trying to get his attention, and then he'd start barking until Danny came over to pet him. Others in the neighborhood noticed how often Danny petted the dog and commented about the special friendship between the man and his four-legged neighbor.

The love between Danny and Crosby is precious, and it is a great reminder of how we so often encounter people in our lives who are looking for someone to care about them, people who need to hear about God's love. Often, it doesn't take much—a few minutes of our time, some wisdom from God's Word shared along the way, or simple acts of compassion for those who have a need. And when we become extensions of God's hands, others will notice.

Lord, help us to love others in the same manner that You love us. Amen.

He Hears My Cry

The righteous cry out, and the LORD hears them;
he delivers them from all their troubles.

PSALM 34:17 NIV

Lucy, my friends' brown and white Beagle, is a beloved part of their family. When Lucy escaped their yard and was hit by a car, Jeff and Sherry thought they would have to say good-bye to her. They took her to the vet, sure they would have to put her down. But the vet thought she could be saved, so Lucy went into surgery and spent several days at the clinic.

Jeff went to pick Lucy up when she was strong enough to come home. After getting instructions about how to take care of her at home, Jeff and the vet headed back to the kennels to fetch Lucy. As soon as Lucy heard Jeff's footsteps she sat up and began whining and crying, begging Jeff to come get her. Surprised, the vet turned to Jeff. "That's the first sound I've heard her make since she's been here," he said. "She didn't whine or bark at all until she heard you." Lucy recognized Jeff was near and cried out, knowing he would hear her and respond. The vet had treated her wounds, but Lucy's relationship with Jeff made her look to him as her source of help.

Just as Lucy recognized Jeff's presence and knew he would come to help her, we can also be confident that God hears us when we cry out to Him. Psalm 34:17 says that when the righteous cry out, the Lord hears them. The righteous are those who enjoy a right relationship with God—something only made possible through Christ. When we come to God for forgiveness of our sins and commit to following Christ Jesus as

Lord, we are made righteous in God's sight. We are no longer strangers, but members of the family of God. And we can be confident that God both hears and responds to the cries of those who call out to Him. His love for us ensures that we are heard.

When we cry out to God, He "delivers us from all our troubles." God's deliverance can come in different forms. Sometimes He removes us from the situation or resolves the conflict for us. Sometimes He gives us the strength we need to persevere and endure. Regardless of the response, we can trust that God sees our needs and is attentive to our cries for help. God does not ignore our pain. "All" means "all." We will never face a difficulty or a situation that God is indifferent to or not strong enough to save us from. God loves us, and He responds to our cries.

Today, if you need help, cry out to the Lord. He hears your cries and will deliver you.

Lord, thank You for hearing my cries and delivering me from all my troubles. When I face trouble, I will look to You as my source of help. Amen.

Understanding Friend

Never let loyalty and kindness leave you!
Tie them around your neck as a reminder.
Write them deep within your heart.

PROVERBS 3:3 NLT

With frazzled nerves, I sat down almost an hour late among mostly strangers at a dinner party in progress. Sadie, a yellow Labrador, placed her chin on my knee and looked up at me with eyes the color of blonde brownies that seemed to say, "It's okay. You're in a safe place now." The precious pet leaned into me, and slowly the knot in my shoulders eased.

Six months earlier, my friends had rescued Sadie from a shelter. They knew little about her previous life, but the dog's timid nature and desire to stay in her crate when she first joined the household lead them to believe the previous owner mistreated her. My friend described her as "the saddest dog I've ever seen."

Labradors have been a constant in my life for over thirty years so the description surprised me. But as I considered how this breed loves their family, I thought maybe the sweet girl still grieved for her previous owner even though this person abandoned her and most likely abused her. It reminds me how sad it must make the Father when His children reject and abandon Him.

Through the first few months, it was heart-lifting to witness Sadie's healing and transformation into a joyful and playful dog. My heart melted when my friend posted a photo of Sadie's first smile. The change in this rescued dog's demeanor didn't happen overnight. It took patience, constant encouragement, love, and plenty of time with her new master.

Sadie also made friends with a former feral cat named Spock. It's interesting, Sadie's new cat-friend never bonded with the other felines in the household, but his affection for the dog was obvious as Spock leaned into Sadie the way she leaned into my thigh and comforted me. My friend speculates that perhaps Spock remembers what it was like to be abandoned and to have no one. Now these two often play, walk, and nap together. Everyone needs a friend and having someone who understood their suffering made all the difference.

God doesn't waste anything. When we learn to forgive those who have hurt us, it becomes a light that leads to the path of healing. And that light of forgiveness can lead others to find healing too. Like a soothing balm, shared understanding and empathy bring comfort and strength to move us into the future. God may bless us with such a friend, but most wonderfully of all, He is always that friend to us.

*Thank You, Father, for the ability to heal in the light
of Your love. Lead me to those who can benefit by hearing
how I've found healing in You and help me
encourage them to love and forgive. Amen.*

The Drive
of Desperation

Suppose you see a brother or sister who has no food or clothing,
and you say, "Good-bye and have a good day;
stay warm and eat well"—but then you don't give that person
any food or clothing. What good does that do?
So you see, faith by itself isn't enough.
Unless it produces good deeds, it is dead and useless.

JAMES 2:15-17 NLT

Fritz had been on the street when he was rescued, although no one knew exactly how long. According to his vet, the young Schnauzer was between two and three years old, and may have been abandoned as a pup. He'd survived by hiding most of the time in an alley and eating whatever he could. He'd lived through more than one beating, and he shied away from most people, barking furiously when anyone got too close.

Finally captured and nurtured back to health, Fritz arrived in his loving, "forever home" still wary and frightened, and the desperation of a life on the streets remained deeply ingrained. Terrified of thunderstorms, he refused to go out in the rain and hid, shivering uncontrollably.

And although Fritz's food bowl was filled on schedule every day, he always acted like it was his last meal, that starvation awaited at any moment. So he never passed up the opportunity to consume what might fill his belly. Anything that hit the floor would be scarfed up and chewed—clothes, shoes, paper, pens. Garbage cans would be ransacked, not just for food scraps but for napkins or tissue as well.

His new owners did what they could to "Fritz-proof" the house, and maintain a constant routine for him, but months passed before Fritz stopped eating anything he could chew and swallow. The habits of desperation were hard to break. Even today, years later, Fritz will still pounce on an unattended tissue and disappear with it. Tissue boxes have to be kept out of the reach of his paws and snout.

Fritz is not alone. Any animal—or person—who goes through a period of severe deprivation will be forever changed. That's one reason God made us stewards not only over the creatures of the earth but our fellow man (see Genesis 1:28; Philippians 2:4; Ephesians 4:32).

Faith is powerful. It should change our behavior as well as our hearts and minds. We were created to uplift and help others, not abandon and abuse. When we put our faith into action we can change the world around us for the better.

Lord, guide me and show me how to put my belief in You and put Your mercy into action. May I encourage and aid those around me, both human and animal, in honor of You and Your creation. Amen.

K-9 Intel

He will rescue you from every trap and protect you
from deadly disease. He will cover you with his feathers.
He will shelter you with his wings. His faithful promises
are your armor and protection.

PSALM 91:3–4 NLT

War bonds soldiers like nothing else, even when the soldier trained to protect you walks on four legs. Specially trained dogs have fought alongside U.S. soldiers in every major war and conflict. Some are trained to sniff out explosives, locate the wounded on the battlefield, or alert soldiers to enemy troops. One German Shepherd named Kobuc, sentry dog of the United States Air Force, earned the title of hero more than four decades ago on a humid battlefield in South Vietnam.

May 23, 1971, started out as any other night. Kobuc, and his handler, Steve, were given orders to guard large tanks of jet fuel housed at the Cam Ranh Bay air base. Twenty-year-old Steve remembers he was excited about returning home on leave soon. But when Kobuc and two other dogs began barking at something in the jungle, his excitement faded. Steve and the other handlers went to investigate. That's when shots rang out and a nearby bomb exploded before it hit the ground. After the second explosion, Kobuc pulled Steve up a hill. "He saved my life on numerous occasions," Steve recalled.

The Viet Cong often used "sappers," elite soldiers armed with explosives, to infiltrate a perimeter and take out key targets. That day Steve counted eight of them before he was able to radio for backup. He didn't know how many grenades and explosive they carried because the enemy was pushed back into the jungle when reinforcements arrived.

If it wasn't for Kobuc and the other dogs, many lives would have been lost that day, and the largest air force base in the area would have suffered great loss. Thankfully, the dogs did their jobs and the crisis was averted.

After all they've been through, Steve will never forget Kobuc. "I still carry his picture in my wallet after all these years," he said.

Kobuc's story demonstrates unwavering loyalty in the face of extreme circumstances. If we look closely, we can catch a glimpse of God's unrelenting faithfulness lived out in His canine creation.

Not unlike the jungles of Vietnam, we face an unseen spiritual enemy and we must rely on God to protects us. When the enemy of our souls wages guerrilla warfare against us, we must stay on alert, suited up in the armor of God, always remembering who fights for us.

Like those on the air base that day, we sometimes feel surrounded and overwhelmed. Those are the days we call for backup, asking friends and family to pray for us. We can trust that God never lets us battle alone.

Jesus, arm me with Your strength for the battle
and help me never forget that You fight for me. Amen.

Patiently Waiting

The LORD is good to those who wait for him,
to the soul who seeks him.

LAMENTATIONS 3:25 ESV

Beth came into the kitchen, eyes half open and a finger extended toward the button on the coffeemaker. Cuff was close at her heels. This was their morning ritual and the twosome could almost carry it out in their sleep.

Beth reached for her mug and as the aroma of the coffee reached her nose, she began to come to life. Cuff, the dog she had rescued only a few years before, wagged his tail and went to sit in his spot by the left cabinet. Cuff knew this was where Beth kept the dog treats and that she would give him his morning treat once she got hers.

Coffee finally in hand, Beth walked over to give Cuff his morning treat then moved to her favorite spot on the screened porch. Sitting in the same spot every morning having quiet time with God made it special, almost sacred. She loved that time and was always disappointed when an early meeting made her miss it.

Glad this was one of her more leisurely mornings, Beth watched the sun come up and took time for a few more sips of her coffee. When she stood to go back down the hall, Cuff went too and took his spot by the cabinet. After pouring another cup, Beth went to her bedroom to get dressed. Once dressed she gathered her work things and headed back to the door. Stopping by the kitchen to get her lunch, Beth found Cuff still sitting by the cabinet, patiently waiting on another treat.

"Cuff, boy! Have you been sitting here all this time waiting for a treat?" Cuff patiently looked up in response. He didn't bark, yip, or jump on her. He just sat.

"Well, we will just have to take care of that." Beth reached for a treat in the cabinet. Cuff continued his patient stance. "Here you go." He opened his mouth and devoured it in one bite.

"I didn't realize you were waiting on me, fella. So sorry to keep you waiting." Beth felt bad about Cuff sitting there so long so she gave him an extra treat. Then, lunch in hand, Beth patted Cuff on the head and started to head out the door.

"You know, Cuff, some days when I am in a hurry I treat God just like I treated you. I go about my business and leave Him waiting for me to finish a conversation or a project. He is patient and waits like you do and eventually I come back. I need you in my life, just like I need God. Thanks for the reminder, Cuff!"

Isn't it amazing to find God patiently waiting for us. We will always find Him nearby, waiting for us to turn to Him no matter how long it takes.

Lord, thank You for Your patience with me.
Help me to keep you waiting less
and to interact more with You. Amen.

Marley's Eyes

*You received God's Spirit when he adopted you
as his own children. Now we call him, "Abba, Father."*

ROMANS 8:15 NLT

I made a friend at the Cave Run Storytelling Festival one year, and his name was Marley. He had the glassiest blue eyes that seemed to pierce right through to my soul. I should mention he also had four legs and a beautiful gray coat of fur.

The festival, held each fall on the shores of Cave Run Lake in Morehead, Kentucky, is one of my favorite events of the year. Top-notch storytellers from around the country perform in a picture-perfect setting, in a big tent with the lake and the fall foliage in the background. I love listening to the stories, but there's something else I like to do at the festival: dog watch. Since it is an outdoor event, many people bring along their dogs—canines in all shapes, sizes, and breeds.

I noticed Marley as I was returning to my seat at the edge of the tent after a break. He and his family were sitting behind me. During one of the performances, I sensed something at my right hand. I looked down, and those stunning blue eyes were peering up at me. Marley had made his way to my chair and nudged my hand, begging for attention. I patted his head and stroked his fur, and he made his home beside me, content as could be.

At intermission, his owner approached me. "I see you've made a friend." He proceeded to tell me the dog's story. Marley, an Australian Shepherd-Poodle mix, was supposed to be a service dog, but things did not go as planned. The original owners didn't bond well with Marley, so this man's family adopted him. With a big smile on his face, the man told me what a blessing Marley had been to him and to his children, and I had to agree. This gentle, sweet dog was my friend for the rest of day, visiting me frequently for some attention.

I imagine Jesus looked upon me with piercing eyes of love when He adopted me into His family. My life was taking twists and turns, and things were not going as I had planned. When I finally approached Jesus and "nudged" Him with my feeble attempt at prayer, He was there with arms wide open. Even though I didn't know much about Him, He met me at the point of my need and rescued me from myself. Life still doesn't always go as I plan, but I am part of a family that shows me love and purpose. Now I can make my home at Jesus's side, as content as Marley was with me at the festival.

Lord, thank You for looking down at me and meeting me where I am. Continue to watch over me. Amen.

Companion
in the Dark

I will ask the Father, and He will give you another Helper,
that He may be with you forever.

JOHN 14:16 NASB

Timothy was the large, furry, well fed and cared for German Shepherd who lived in our subdivision where I grew up. Whenever I saw Timothy, he always—always—had a ball in his slobbery mouth. Timothy would drop the ball at my feet, or anyone else's feet, sit patiently, and wait for the ball to be thrown. He'd chase it and return, tail wagging, to continue the game as long as possible.

Every time there was enough snow for sledding, the street Timothy lived on was left unplowed. Whenever that happened, Timothy was out there with the rest of us having himself a grand ole time, chasing snowballs and following sleds down the hill.

One evening when I was in elementary school, my junior-high brother and I went sledding down Timothy's street. After a while, my hands, feet, and nose were numb and I wanted to go home. Bob, however, did not. I knew my way home. It wasn't far. But it was dark. I'd never walked that far in the dark by myself before and I didn't want to start now. When I couldn't persuade Bob to leave, I hesitantly ventured out on my own, praying as I went.

I hadn't gone far when I sensed I was being followed. Before I knew it, something large bumped up against me and leaned into my side. Timothy. I'd never been so happy to see that dog. I talked with Timothy the whole way home. He was my companion. He was my protector. He was my friend. When I reached my house, I hugged Timothy with all my might and thanked him for getting me home safe.

When I walked away from my brother that night and told him I could get home fine on my own, thank you very much, I wasn't so sure I could actually do it. Fortunately for me, Timothy came along, and with him by my side I didn't have to walk home in the dark alone.

Before Jesus left this earth and returned to His home in heaven, He told His disciples He would send them a Comforter—He would send them someone to walk alongside them as they traveled through life. The Holy Spirit would be their guide and protect them. They didn't need to be afraid for the Holy Spirit would always be with them, even in the dark when they walked home alone. The same is true for us.

Whenever the things of this world frighten us and we feel all alone, we need to remember we aren't walking home by ourselves. The Holy Spirit is right there with us. He comforts and keeps us safe even through the darkest night.

Jesus, thank You for sending Your Holy Spirit to walk through life with us to make sure we are never alone when we travel through the dark. Amen.

Learning to Wait

If we hope for what we do not yet have,
we wait for it patiently.

ROMANS 8:25 NIV

The postcard addressed to our son Daniel puzzled me. It read: "Thank you for saving Darryl's life. It's people like you who make a difference in the world." Who in the world was Darryl? And how did Daniel save his life?

We soon found out. Without telling us, Daniel adopted Darryl from a humane society in the city where he lived four hours away. We soon adopted him too as our very first grand-dog. Darryl turned out to be the fastest, strongest dog I've ever met. His speed and strength made him nearly impossible to control in his early years. "Wait!" was the hardest command for Darryl to follow. Walking him on a leash was out of the question unless one's shoulder sockets needed a major realignment.

Ever eager, Darryl's entire body quivered and his tail thumped wildly with anticipation when anyone approached a door with the prospect of opening it. He perpetuated constant motion, hurling himself down the steps with such excruciating squeals and hurricane force that those in his path better hold on for dear life. The trouble was, we lived only yards from a busy road, so Darryl's darting about with no discipline was quite dangerous. Many times when he was in our care I prayed he would not be run over.

Of course, Darryl possessed endearing qualities, too. Those perky pointy ears, broad chest, "wrinkly skin," upturned tail, black toenails—all part of a "fine canine blend"—made his breed somewhat hard to determine. But there was no question about his energy or enthusiasm. His eyes shone with eagerness and adoration whenever he heard his master's voice or footsteps. Though not in his nature, over time he learned to please Daniel by waiting for permission to go out or to eat a treat only when given the "Okay!" signal. To our surprise, Darryl began to contain his energy and obey commands. The only reward he needed was a "Good boy" and a pat on the head. Then he settled contentedly beside Daniel's chair with only eyes and tail in motion until Daniel decided to move again.

Watching Darryl's transformation reminds me of how I need to learn to wait upon my Master. How often have I run ahead of my loving Father's command, so eager to experience the delights of the world that I failed to heed His warnings? After all, open doorways may beckon us to freedom yet fail to reveal dangers or disillusionment waiting just down the steps or around the corner. I want to work on my waiting skills, especially when I'm hoping for something or someone in my future to fulfill a need or desire. God knows best. I trust Him. Like Darryl, I will learn to wait for my Master's "Okay!"

Father, thank You for patiently teaching us to wait
for Your perfect timing and Your perfect will. Amen.

It's a Dog's Life

Do not be anxious about your life, what you will eat or what you
will drink, nor about your body, what you will put on.
Is not life more than food, and the body more than clothing?
Look at the birds of the air: they neither sow nor reap
nor gather into barns, and yet your heavenly Father feeds them.

MATTHEW 6:25-26 ESV

Sadie, our white and tan, mixed-breed bird dog, lay on the living room rug, absolutely content with the world. "Oh, the life of a dog," Judy sighed. "I wish someone took care of me and bought me food so I could sleep easy."

The heads in the room nodded in unison as everyone turned to gaze at the snoozing dog. Every now and then Sadie lifted up one eyelid, but mostly she relaxed, not a care in the world. And why would she have a care?

Every morning Sadie walks near a park and receives praise from children who scratch behind her ears and stroke her neck. Most afternoons you can find her underneath the peach tree, resting in its shade. In the evenings, she takes long strolls around the lake where she chases rabbits or takes a swim. Besides being well-fed and exercised, Sadie seems to share a house with a live-in maid and butler who pick up after her and groom her. Dogs really do have it good, don't they?

If you've ever envied the stress-free life of your dog, you've probably let worry and anxiety creep into your life. But here's the good news: We have a Master who takes care of us, and His care far outweighs the care of even the most pampered pets.

When we bring our lives into mastery under Jesus's control, we don't need to worry about daily life. This is not to say we quit working and lounge around, but we take on our daily ventures with confidence. Jesus even gave a lesson on anxiety by showing the carefree nature of birds. Birds and dogs never worry about where their next meal will come from. They don't sweat it when the mailbox yields an unexpected medical (or vet) bill. Dogs patiently wait for their master to provide all their needs. They live fully present in the moment.

Likewise, God wants us to live fully present with Him as He is fully present with us. To surrender our hearts in worship like this, we must lay aside worry. A heart can either be occupied in worry or worship. It cannot do both.

Learning how to live in God's presence requires our full reliance on Him, much the same way our beloved dogs rely on us. Our lives matter so much more to Him than we can conceive and He promises to meet our every need.

Lord Jesus, teach me to rely on You
and not fret about daily life; I place my life in Your hands,
knowing that You truly care about me. Amen.

THANK YOU
TO OUR CONTRIBUTORS

Michelle Medlock Adams
Rachel Britton
Heather Creekmore
Michelle Cox
Linda Gilden
Carlton Hughes
Trish Mugo
Diane Nunley
Dalene Parker
Dee Dee (Michelle) Parker
Leigh Powers
Sandy Kirby Quandt
Ramona Richards
Shelia Stovall
Tammy Van Gils

IF YOU ENJOYED THIS BOOK, WILL YOU CONSIDER SHARING THE MESSAGE WITH OTHERS?

Mention the book in a blog post or through Facebook, Twitter, Pinterest, or upload a picture through Instagram.

Recommend this book to those in your small group, book club, workplace, and classes.

Head over to facebook.com/worthypublishing, "LIKE" the page, and post a comment as to what you enjoyed the most.

Tweet "I recommend reading #SoGodMadeADog by @worthypub"

Pick up a copy for someone you know who would be challenged and encouraged by this message.

Write a book review online.

Visit us at worthypublishing.com

twitter.com/worthypub

worthypub.tumblr.com

facebook.com/worthypublishing

pinterest.com/worthypub

instagram.com/worthypub

youtube.com/worthypublishing